1

HISTORICAL COMPUTING VOLUME III: Programming Matrices and Polynomials

BY

Dr. Peta Trigger Ph.D, Ed.D

K B P

2 Emms Hill Barns

Hamsterley

County Durham

First published 2014

ISBN 9781495399183

PRINTED BY CREATESPACE

https://www.createspace.com

FOREWORD

This volume describes the development computer programs in *Borland TurboC* using the *BASIC* of the 1980's as used on the 'micro-computers' (the forerunners of 'PC's) of the period. The purpose has twofold aspects. The first is to show the usefulness of *BASIC* in initially writing programs which would *work*, as a stepping stone onto the harder programming in the 'C' versions. The second is to take much of the labour out of solving problems in Engineering Science involving the inversion of matrices with complex elements; solving higher order simultaneous equations, and solving higher order polynomial equations. All the final programs run on modern *Windows* computers.

TABLE OF CONTENTS

4

6

8

9

10

LIST OF FIGURES

INTRODUCTION

For each of the programs to be described, examples of the mathematical problems which it is designed to solve are given before describing how the main aspects of the program perform the mathematical operations involved. This book is a *programming* work, which therefore makes use of the *results* of prior mathematical analysis. Readers interested the *derivation* of these results used here will find a full treatment in a *mathematical* work in Trigger (2013). Examples of the types of problems in engineering science which the programs may be used to solve are also described, along with descriptions of how the programs may be used to solve them in specific cases.

Each program provides the user with a check on the truth and accuracy of the result or solution found:

In the matrix inversion program, the inverted matrix found by the program is multiplied by the original matrix to determine how close the product comes to the identity matrix;

in the simultaneous equations-solving program, the solution found by the program is substituted into the set of simultaneous equations, and the r.h.s. are calculated to determine how close they come to the constants inputted to the program;

in the polynomial equation-solving program, the roots found in the program are substituted into the polynomial equation to determine how close the result comes to zero.

DEVELOPING THE PROGRAMS

1. THE *BASIC* PROGRAMMING ENVIRONMENT

The *BASIC* programs, after typing the program into a computer running *BASIC*, are executed directly simply by entering the RUN instruction. Here, the AMSTRAD PCW256 was used. However, the *BASIC* interpreter Vintbas.exe complete with editable *BASIC* files can be also be used to advantage. The use of this modern programming environment based on late 1970's and 80's *BASIC* is fully explained in Volume I of this series.

Vintbas enables the *BASIC* programs developed here to be run and modified on *Windows*-based computers. One of the editable files supplied with Vintbas.exe can be opened in Notepad and the program code substituted for the code in the editable file. It should then be saved as a **.bas** file, as say cadjinv.bas if the code for the above complex matrix inversion program was used. For debugging, the file name of the *BASIC* program under development should be entered at the command prompt so that the developer is notified of the type of errors found and their line numbers:

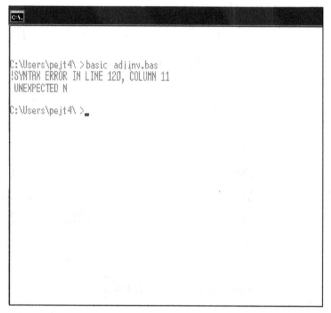

```
C:\Users\pejt4\ >basic adjinv.bas
!SYNTAX ERROR IN LINE 120, COLUMN 11
 UNEXPECTED N

C:\Users\pejt4\ >_
```

The debugger in *Vintbas*

2. THE *TURBOC* PROGRAMMING ENVIRONMENT

The 'C' programs need a C development environment to compile the C program, link in the 'library' files used in the program (which, for example, read characters from the keyboard or display characters on the screen) and produce an executable file. The Borland C v2.01 programming package also contains a debugger. This is shown below:

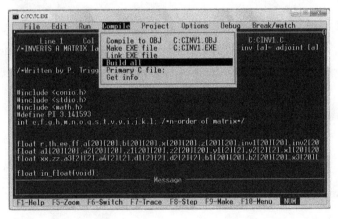

With the C program loaded into the debugger, the program can be executed by selecting an option from the drop-down menus as shown to 'build all'- that is compile, link and make an executable file.

This can then be run as follows:

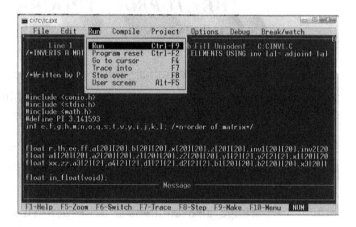

For editing c files, the G.U.I. (Graphics User Interface) PFE editor is more convenient to use than the C.L. Command Line Interface) Borland *turboC* debugger. This is shown below:

```
┌──────────────────────────────────────────────────────────────────────────────┐
│ [icons]                              │ 1 Compile                              │
│                                      │ 2 Compile and link                     │
│ /*INVERTS A MATRIX [a] CO┤           │ 3 Compile, link and run    ]/det [a] */│
│                                      │ 4 Run                                  │
│ /*Written by P. Trigger*/            │                                        │
│                                                                                │
│ #include <conio.h>                                                             │
│ #include <stdio.h>                                                             │
│ #include <math.h>                                                              │
│ #define PI 3.141593                                                            │
│ int e,f,g,h,m,n,o,q,s,t,v,                                                     │
│                                                                                │
│ Float r,th,ee,FF,a[20][20],b[20][20],x[20][20],z[20][20],inv1[20][20],inv2[20][20];/*a?[][] is input matrix, inv?[][ │
│ Float a1[20][20],a2[20][20],z1[20][20],z2[20][20],y1[2][2],y2[2][2],x1[20][20],x2[20][20]; │
│ Float xx,zz,a3[2][2],aa[2][2],d1[2][2],d2[2][2],b1[20][20],b2[20][20],x3[20][20],x4[20][20],aa,bb,cc,dd; │
│                                                                                │
│ Float in_Float(void);                                                          │
│ int in_int(void);                                                              │
│ void evaluate_determinant(void);                                               │
│ void swop_rows(void);                                                          │
│ void put_x_in_a(void);                                                          │
│ void flush_array(void);                                                         │
│ void multiply_matrices(void);                                                  │
│                                                                                │
│ void evaluate_determinant_divisor(void);                                       │
│ void _elemult(void);                                                           │
│ void _kthroot(void);                                                           │
│                                                                                │
│ main()                                                                         │
│        {                                                                       │
│        cprintf("Written by P. Trigger\r\n\n\n");                               │
│        cprintf("An example in the use of the program\r\n\n\n");                │
│        cprintf("Consider the matrix:\r\n\n\n");                                 │
│        cprintf("1+2j   3+4j\r\n\n");                                            │
│        cprintf("5+6j   7+8j\r\n\n");                                            │
│        cprintf("The order of the matrix to be inverted is 2\r\n\n");           │
│        cprintf("The REAL part of the element in row 1 column 1 is 1, imaginary part 2\r\n\n"); │
│        cprintf("The REAL part of the element in row 1 column 2 is 3, imaginary part 4\r\n\n"); │
│        cprintf("The REAL part of the element in row 2 column 1 is 5, imaginary part 6\r\n\n"); │
└──────────────────────────────────────────────────────────────────────────────┘
```

PFE GUI Editor

1. THE DEVELOPMENT OF A COMPUTER PROGRAM TO INVERT MATRICES WITH COMPLEX ELEMENTS

Background

INTRODUCTION

The aim of this introduction is to show in outline how to find the voltages and currents in the circuit using a method involving multiplication of transmission matrices (more details are given in Trigger, *op. cit.*).

The transmission matrix of special interest here, is a 2 x 2 (i.e. 2 rows and 2 columns) matrix with elements representing resistances, conductances, impedances or admittances.

Consider the A.C. circuit in Fig. 1 below:

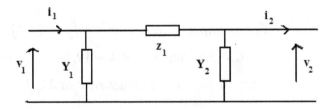

FIG 1: AN A.C. CIRCUIT

The input/output voltages and currents of this

circuit are given by the product of the transmission matrices for each of the three stages of the circuit:

$$
\begin{bmatrix} v_1 \\ i_1 \end{bmatrix} = \begin{bmatrix} 1 & 0 \\ Y_1 & 1 \end{bmatrix} \begin{bmatrix} 1 & z_1 \\ 0 & 1 \end{bmatrix} \begin{bmatrix} 1 & 0 \\ Y_2 & 1 \end{bmatrix} \begin{bmatrix} v_2 \\ i_2 \end{bmatrix}
$$

which, when values are assigned to the admittances and impedances, will contain complex elements.

The above equation is derived from first principles using current and voltage laws and the elementary properties of matrices in Trigger *op. cit.*

FINDING THE OUTPUT VOLTAGE AND CURRENT FROM THE INPUT VOLTAGE AND CURRENT

For example, Y_1 might be $3 + 1j$; z_1 $2 - 4j$; Y_2 $5 - 3j$; v_1 $-6 - 3.8j$ and i_1 $-14.4 - 19.1j$, with appropriate units. What are the values of v_2 and i_2 ?

In answer to questions like this in engineering science using transmission matrices, a computer program to invert the resulting product matrix with complex elements is required if tedious hand methods are to be avoided. Such a program will be developed here from first principles, which is capable not only of inverting 2x2 complex matrices, but 3x3, 4x4, ... order matrices.

THE APPROACH USED IN DEVELOPING THE PROGRAM

The rule for addition of matrices allows us to split a complex matrix into a matrix with real coefficients and a matrix with imaginary coefficients, which greatly facilitates programming. Thus, if when the three transmission matrices are multiplied out, the product is:

$$
\begin{bmatrix} a + ib & c + id \\ e + if & g + ih \end{bmatrix}
$$

then

$$
\begin{bmatrix} a + ib & c + id \\ e + if & g + ih \end{bmatrix} = \begin{bmatrix} a & c \\ e & g \end{bmatrix} + i \begin{bmatrix} b & d \\ f & h \end{bmatrix}
$$

Hence, the first step is to develop a method of inverting matrices with real elements only, which can then be extended to encompass matrices with the addition of imaginary components to these real entries.

A METHOD OF INVERTING MATRICES WITH REAL ELEMENTS ONLY

The method used here is preferred for its overt use of matrix algebra to invert the matrix itself, and because it is straightforwardly extended to matrices with complex elements. It involves determinants and their evaluation by successive reduction to determinants of lower order, ending up with a 2nd order determinant which can easily be expanded.

If A is the matrix to be inverted $|A|$ =det A its determinant and adj$A$ the adjoint matrix of A, then

$$A^{-1} = |A|^{-1}.adjA$$

The above equation is derived from first principles and the elementary properties of determinants and matrices in Trigger *op. cit.*

PROGRAMMING THE METHOD

The method was first programmed in *BASIC* running on an Amstrad PCW 8256. The successful programming techniques developed in *BASIC* were then used to write a Borland Turbo 'C' program version to run on *Windows* computers.

The method was first programmed in *BASIC* for its ease of use, enabling the author to concentrate on programming the method without getting too bogged down with difficulties of translating it into the more complex code of the 'C' programming environment. Debugging was also easier because partially developed programs/subroutines could be isolated and executed directly.

Once all the problems in getting the program to run properly were solved, the subroutines used could be re-programmed in 'C', simplifying the writing of the more important version (because more portable between modern computers and faster) of the program which would run on DOS-based computers.

SIMPLIFYING PROGRAMMING BY SPLITTING A COMPLEX MATRIX INTO REAL AND IMAGINARY MATRICES

A complex matrix can be split into two real matrices, the second multiplied by i. Hence to start with a *BASIC* program was developed to invert matrices with real elements only, which could then be extended to invert matrices containing complex elements.

DEVELOPING THE *BASIC* MATRIX INVERSION PROGRAM

In performing the two main operations of the mathematics of the method used to invert a matrix outlined above, the program consists of two main subroutines: one to evaluate a determinant, the other to build an adjoint matrix, adj$\mathbf{A}$, from the matrix to be inverted, $\mathbf{A}$.

Other parts of the program are concerned with such processes as:

(1) inputting the values of the matrix elements from the keyboard and storing them in appropriate arrays;

(2) printing out the input and output matrices;

(3) Finding the product $\mathbf{A}.\mathbf{A}^{-1}$ to check that the result is close to $\mathbf{I}$.

The programming of these processes is fairly straightforward and will not be discussed in detail here, though the routines involved can be viewed in the printout of the finished program in Appendix7.

However, the subroutines for calculating the value of $|A|$ and adj$A$ will be considered in some detail next.

THE SUBROUTINE FOR CALCULATING |A|

This is shown beginning at line 620 in the BASIC program printout. The first requirement is that the element $1,1 = a_1$ is non-zero, since this is used as a divisor. Called at line 650, the subroutine at line 830 swaps adjacent rows to bring the largest absolute value of the first element in any row into the 'pivotal' position $(i,j)=(1,1)$. The resulting sign change to the value of the determinant is held in the variable x at line 870, having been initialized to 1 at line 630.

Line 690 generates the 2nd order determinants or 'minors' which become the elements of the condensed matrix. **A**, the inputted matrix, is stored in a(. , .), so the leading element of each condensed matrix is in a(1,1).

The first element of the condensed matrix, with i=1, j=1, is therefore

a(1,1)*a(2,2) - a(2,1)*a(1,2).

The next element of the condensed matrix in row 1 is produced by incrementing j to j=2, repeating the above calculation with the new values of i and j.

This procedure is continued until the first row of elements of the condensed matrix is complete, then i is incremented to i=2, and the 2nd row of elements is produced in like fashion, continuing until all $(n-1)^2$ elements of the condensed determinant have been generated.

This n-1th order determinant is next condensed to a n-2nd order determinant, then n-3rd and so on, ending when a 2nd order determinant is reached, which is easily evaluated as a cross-product. This is the function of the instruction in line 640, together with the associated 'next k' instruction.

Each element of the condensed determinant is stored in   x(. , .) in line 690. Each condensed *determinant* is multiplied by $1/a^{k-1}$ (where k is the order of the 1st condensed determinant), by multiplying each *element* by $(1/a^{k-1})^{1/k}$ (if this is not done, products may become so large that an overflow error results), since for a determinant $|M|$ of order p multiplied by coefficient y,

$$y.|M| = |y^{1/k}.M|.$$

This procedure is carried out at lines 770 and 785.

THE SUBROUTINE FOR DETERMINING THE ELEMENTS OF adjA

First, at line 330, the value of $|A|$ in $x(1,1)$ at exit from the determinant evaluating subroutine, is held in d. The subroutine for adjA begins at line 350.

$z(.\,,.)$ contains the elements of **A** and the cofactor of element u,v of **A** is in $a(s,t)$ at line 440. Lines 410 and 420 ensure that elements in the same row and column u,v of **A** are omitted as required.

Each cofactor, a determinant of order one less than its parent determinant, is evaluated by the subroutine at line 620. Line 510 transposes these values, held in the array inv $(.\,,.)$, simply by swapping the order of the row and column suffices u and v, forming the adjoint matrix. Each element of the adjoint matrix is divided by $d = |A|$, attaching the correct sign by multiplying by $(-1)^{u+v}$.

The subroutine at line 540 prints out the inverted matrix whose elements are in inv (v,u).

EXTENDING THE METHOD TO MATRICES WITH COMPLEX ELEMENTS

multiplying complex numbers

The methods for condensing determinants and generating adjoint matrices, which are the crux of the method used here for inverting matrices, involve taking the products of elements. If these elements are complex numbers, then in general their products will be complex numbers.

Generally, if the element $a + ib$ is multiplied by the element $c + id$, where a, b, c and d are real numbers, then

$$(a + ib)(c + id) = ac - bd + i(bc + ad).$$

MODIFYING THE EXPRESSION FOR CROSS PRODUCTS IN THE PROGRAM FOR REAL MATRICES TO CATER FOR COMPLEX ELEMENTS

We have

$$
\begin{vmatrix}
a_{11} + ib_{11} & a_{1,j+1} + ib_{1,j+1} \\
a_{i+1,1} + ib_{i+1,1} & a_{i+1,j+1} + ib_{i+1,j+1}
\end{vmatrix}
$$

$$
=
$$

$$
a_{1,1}a_{i+1,j+1} + i(b_{1,1}a_{i+1,j+1} + a_{1,1}b_{i+1,j+1}) - b_{1,1}b_{i+1,j+1} -
$$
$$
[a_{1,j+1}a_{i+1,1} + i(b_{i,j+1}a_{i+1,1} + a_{1,j+1}b_{i+1,1}) - b_{1,j+1}b_{i+1,1}]
$$

REAL PARTS OF THE CONDENSED DETERMINANT ELEMENTS: DETERMINANT EVALUATION SUBROUTINE

If the elements are real only (coefficients $b = 0$), then the above expression reduces to

$$a_{1,1}a_{i+1,j+1} - a_{1,j+1}a_{i+1,1} .$$

In Appendix 7, we can see that this is precisely the expression in line 690.

If the b coefficients are not zero, then two further real-valued terms need to be added to this expression viz.:

$$- b_{1,1}b_{i+1,j+1} \text{ and } b_{1,j+1}b_{i+1,1} .$$

In the program extended to deal with matrices with complex elements in Appendix 8, line 1060 shows the complete expression for the real part of each element of the condensed determinant, noting that a1 is used in place of a and a2 in place of b in the above expression.

IMAGINARY PARTS OF THE CONDENSED DETERMINANT ELEMENTS

From the foregoing, the expression for the imaginary part is

$$b_{1,1}a_{i+1,j+1} + a_{1,1}b_{i+1,j+1} - b_{i,j+1}a_{i+1,1} - a_{1,j+1}b_{i+1,1}.$$

With a1 used in place of a and a2 in place of b, this is the expression in line 1070 in Appendix 8.

The real parts thus produced are held in one array X1(. , .) and the imaginary parts are held in X2(. , .).

DIVISION OF COMPLEX NUMBERS

Generally, we have

$$\frac{a + ib}{c + id} = \frac{ac + cd}{c^2 + d^2} + i \frac{bc - ad)}{c^2 + d^2}$$

MODIFYING THE ADJOINT MATRIX SUBROUTINE

In the program to invert real matrices in Appendix 7, line 510 divides the evaluated cofactor (which is itself a determinant, it will be remembered) by the value of the determinant of the to-be-inverted matrix, i.e., |A| (=d). The evaluated cofactor is stored in X(1,1).

In the extended program, we have in addition an imaginary part for each cofactor and an imaginary part for |A|: X1(1,1), X2(1,1) and d1 and d2, respectively.

Hence substituting X1 and a1 for a and c and X2 and d2 for b and d in equation (1) above, the required expressions replacing that in line 510 in the real matrix inversion program are:

$$\frac{X1.d1 + X2.d2}{d1^2 + d2^2}$$

for the real part and

$$\frac{X2.d1 - X1.d2}{d1^2 + d2^2}$$

for the imaginary part.

These are shown in line 600 and line 610 in the extended program in Appendix 8.

THE SUBROUTINE FOR FINDING THE ROOT OF AN IMAGINARY NUMBER

The method used to invert a matrix involves multiplying a condensed determinant by the factor $1/a_{11}^{n-2}$, where a_{11} is the leading element of $|A|$, or $1/a_{11}^{k-1}$, where k is the order of the condensed matrix.

This in turn requires each element of the condensed determinant of order k to be multiplied by the kth root of the multiplier, i.e.,

$$\left[\frac{1}{a_{11}^{k-1}} \right]^{1/k}$$

.

However, in general, the multiplier for a determinant with complex elements will itself be complex and so a new subroutine is required to find the kth root of an imaginary number.

The real part of the kth root of a + ib is
$r^{1/k}.\cos Th$

and the imaginary part is
$r^{1/k}.\sin Th$.

where $\mathrm{Th} = 1/k \cdot \tan^{-1} \left[\dfrac{\sqrt{1 - (a^2/r^2)}}{a/r} \right]$

(Trigger, *op. cit.*)

THE COMPLEX ROOT-FINDING
SUBROUTINE

With Y1 and Y2 substituted for a and b, this is the essence of the subroutine which finds the kth root of a complex number (the particular complex numbers being fed to the subroutine being the condensed determinants multipliers) at line 8000 in Appendix 8.

The *BASIC* syntax used in writing the *BASIC* programs in described in Appendix 5.

RE-WRITING THE *BASIC* PROGRAM IN BORLAND TURBO 'C' FOR *WINDOWS* COMPUTERS

Having found that initially tackling a program in *BASIC* to invert matrices with real elements only considerably eased the problem writing the complex matrix inverting program, a similar procedure was adopted for the program in 'C'.

The program inverting matrices with complex elements in 'C' is shown in Appendix 1 (The 'C' version of the real matrix-inverting program is not considered here. As in the case of the BASIC program the imaginary matrix-inverting program in 'C' subsumes the real matrix-inverting program and therefore can also invert matrices with real elements or a mix of elements by entering appropriate imaginary components as 0's).

The structure of the program in terms of subroutines, for example to evaluate a determinant is shown in Appendix 1, and the subroutine to generate the adjoint matrix is also shown.

The writing of the code was made much easier having worked out the logic behind each instruction in each subroutine before hand in *BASIC*.

The main additional requirements of programming in the new language over *BASIC* were:

(1) Subroutines called from the main program had to be declared at the outset in print statements (see Appendix 1);

(2) Integer values and floating point values also had to be declared before they were used (see Appendix 1);

(3) Array sizes used to hold matrices and determinants had to be declared before the start of the main program (the code starting with 'main' in Appendix 1);

(4) The nesting of for/next loops enclosed in curly brackets which therefore figure throughout the program;

(5) Two subroutines were written to input integer and floating point values from the keyboard (function in_int() and in_float()). Other specially written subroutines to clear the values in an array (flush_array), to fill a new array with the elements of an existing array (put_x_in_a) and the functions

of evaluate_determinant_divisor and elemult are briefly explained by comments in the program.

Of course, a number of arithmetic and print statements differ in 'C' from those in *BASIC*, and so the latter had to be 'translated'. For example, printing out the value of the element a, a(i,j) in *BASIC* is accomplished by the instruction

print a(i,j),

whereas in 'C' the required form is

cprintf("%f",a[i][j])

if the element is a floating-point number.

The syntax used in the 'c' programs is described in Appendix 6.

Apart from these changes, writing the 'C' program to invert matrices with complex elements presented no special problems after writing the program in *BASIC*.

APPLICATION OF THE PROGRAM TO A PRACTICAL PROBLEM IN ENGINEERING SCIENCE

Consider the 'π' network in Fig. 2, on p. 51. Suppose Y_1 is $3 + 1j$ (engineers use 'j' in preference to 'i' for

$\sqrt{-1}$ since i is used for current) z_1 is $2 - 4j$,

that v_1 is $-6 - 3.8j$ and i_1 is $-14.4 - 19.1j$, with appropriate units.

Inserting these values into the appropriate matrices:

$$\begin{bmatrix} -6 & -3.8j \\ -14.4 & -19.1j \end{bmatrix} = \begin{bmatrix} 1+0j & 0+0j \\ 3+1j & 1+0j \end{bmatrix} \begin{bmatrix} 1+0j & 2-4j \\ 0+0j & 1+0j \end{bmatrix} \begin{bmatrix} 1+0j & 0+0j \\ 5-3j & 1+0j \end{bmatrix} \begin{bmatrix} v_2 \\ i_2 \end{bmatrix}$$

The C file which multiplies matrices of any order is in Appendix 4 . Using this matrix multiplication program:

```
C:\.

Enter the number of rows of the first matrix2
Enter the number of columns of the first matrix2

Enter element in row 1 column 1 Real part
1

Enter element in row 1 column 1 Imaginary part
0

Enter element in row 1 column 2 Real part
0

Enter element in row 1 column 2 Imaginary part
0

Enter element in row 2 column 1 Real part
3

Enter element in row 2 column 1 Imaginary part
1

Enter element in row 2 column 2 Real part

1

Enter element in row 2 column 2 Imaginary part
0
Enter the number of rows of the second matrix2
Enter the number of columns of the second matrix2

Enter element in row 1 column 1 Real part
1

Enter element in row 1 column 1 Imaginary part
0

Enter element in row 1 column 2 Real part
2

Enter element in row 1 column 2 Imaginary part
-4

Enter element in row 2 column 1 Real part
0

Enter element in row 2 column 1 Imaginary part
0
```

```
Enter element in row 2 column 2 Real part
1

Enter element in row 2 column 2 Imaginary part
0
Matrix [a] is;

1.000000 j0.000000  0.000000 j0.000000
3.000000 j1.000000  1.000000 j0.000000

Matrix [b] is;

1.000000 j0.000000  2.000000 j-4.000000
0.000000 j0.000000  1.000000 j0.000000


Product matrix is;

1.000000 j0.000000  2.000000 j-4.000000
3.000000 j1.000000  11.000000 j-10.000000
-

Multiply result by another matrix (y/n)?
Enter the number of rows of the second matrix2
Enter the number of columns of the second matrix2

Enter element in row 1 column 1 Real part
1

Enter element in row 1 column 1 Imaginary part
0

Enter element in row 1 column 2 Real part
0

Enter element in row 1 column 2 Imaginary part
0

Enter element in row 2 column 1 Real part
5

Enter element in row 2 column 1 Imaginary part
-3
```

```
Enter element in row 2 column 2 Real part
1
Enter element in row 2 column 2 Imaginary part
0
Matrix [a] is;

1.000000 j0.000000  2.000000 j-4.000000
3.000000 j1.000000  11.000000 j-10.000000

Matrix [b] is;

1.000000 j0.000000  0.000000 j0.000000
5.000000 j-3.000000  1.000000 j0.000000


Product matrix is;

-1.000000 j-26.000000  2.000000 j-4.000000
28.000000 j-82.000000  11.000000 j-10.000000
```

gives:

$$\begin{bmatrix} -1 - 26j & 2 - 4j \\ 28 - 82j & 11 - 10j \end{bmatrix}$$

Using the matrix inversion program:

```
0.375-0.3125j   -0.125+0.0625j

Enter the order of the matrix to be inverted2

Enter the REAL part of the element in row 1 column 1
-1

Enter the IMAGINARY part of the element in row 1 column 1
-26

Enter the REAL part of the element in row 1 column 2
2

Enter the IMAGINARY part of the element in row 1 column 2
-4

Enter the REAL part of the element in row 2 column 1
28

Enter the IMAGINARY part of the element in row 2 column 1
-82

Enter the REAL part of the element in row 2 column 2
11

Enter the IMAGINARY part of the element in row 2 column 2
-10
The matrix [a] to be inverted is;

-1.000000 j-26.000000 2.000000 j-4.000000
28.000000 j-82.000000 11.000000 j-10.000000

Inverted matrix is;

11.000000 j-10.000000 -2.000000 j4.000000
-28.000000 j82.000000 -1.000000 j-26.000000


Check by calculating product of input matrix and its calculated inverse

1.000000 j0.000000 0.000000 j0.000000
0.000000 j0.000000 1.000000 j0.000000
```

gives:

$$\begin{bmatrix} 11 - 10j & -2 + 4j \\ -28 + 82j & -1 - 26j \end{bmatrix}$$

In this case, the elements in the inverted matrix are transpositions of the elements of the original matrix (with changes of sign) because of the $1 + 0j$'s in the diagonals of the multiplicands.

Multiplying the inverted matrix by

$$\begin{bmatrix} -6 & -3.8j \\ -14.4 & -19.1j \end{bmatrix}$$

gives

$$\begin{bmatrix} v_2 \\ \\ i_2 \end{bmatrix} = \begin{bmatrix} 1.2 - 1.2j \\ \\ -2.6 + 7.9j \end{bmatrix}$$

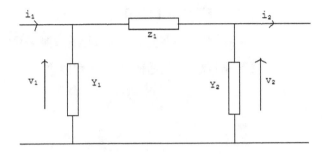

Fig 2: A 'π' NETWORK CONSISTING OF AN
IMPEDANCE AND TWO ADMITTANCES

2. THE DEVELOPMENT OF A COMPUTER PROGRAM TO SOLVE HIGHER ORDER SIMULTANEOUS EQUATIONS FOR USE IN PROBLEMS IN ENGINEERING SCIENCE

INTRODUCTION

Consider the circuit in Fig. 3 in where the problem is to find the unknown voltages $v_2 - v_5$:

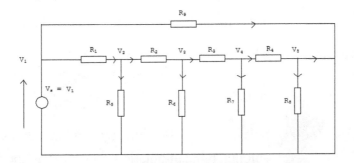

Fig. 3: A CIRCUIT CONSISTING OF RESISTANCES AND A VOLTAGE SOURCE

$$-(R_2R_5 + R_1R_5 + R_1R_2)v_2 + R_1R_5v_3 = -R_2R_5v_1 \quad (5)$$

$$R_3R_6v_2 - (R_3R_6 + R_2R_6 + R_2R_3)v_3 + R_2R_6v_4 = 0 \quad (6).$$

$$R_4R_7v_3 - (R_4R_7 + R_3R_7 + R_4R_3)v_3 + R_3R_7v_5 = 0 \quad (7).$$

and

$$R_4R_8v_1 - (R_4R_8 + R_8R_9 + R_4R_8)v_5 + R_4R_9v_4 = 0 \quad (8).$$

If $v_1 = v_s$ is known, we have 4 simultaneous equations in 4 unknowns. If R_1 - R_9 are known, we have four equations of the form:

$$au_1 + bu_2 + cu_3 + du_4 = \text{constant,}$$

where u_1, u_2, u_3 and u_4 represent the unknowns, here the voltages v_2 - v_5, and a, b, c, and d the coefficients of the unknowns, which here are products of resistance values and some may be zero.

Solving these equations by hand is tedious, and the amount of manipulation increases as the order of the set of simultaneous equations increases.

Even if simple values of coefficients are involved, mistakes in the arithmetical calculations inevitably increase the labour of finding a solution. With more realistic valued coefficients (which it will be remembered are products of resistance values in the circuit example), greater likelihood of error and more awkward fractions will be involved.

The method of solving simultaneous equations to be used in the program is a matrix one, which follows naturally from the work of developing the program to invert matrices described previously.

SOLVING SIMULTANEOUS EQUATIONS USING ADJOINT MATRICES AND DETERMINANTS

From the previous work, the inverse of a matrix is given by

$\mathbf{A}^{-1} = |A|^{-1}.\text{adj}\mathbf{A}.$

Let **A** be the matrix of coefficients of the unknowns, **x** the column matrix of unknowns and **k** the column matrix of r.h.s. constants.

Then the set of equations is

$\mathbf{A}\mathbf{x} = \mathbf{k}$

and the solution is given by

$\mathbf{x} = \mathbf{A}^{-1}\mathbf{k}$.

In the case of a set of 4 equations in four unknowns

$x_1 , x_2 , x_3 , x_4 ,$

we therefore have:

$$x_1 = \frac{\begin{vmatrix} k_1 & a_{12} & a_{13} & a_{14} \\ k_2 & a_{22} & a_{23} & a_{24} \\ k_3 & a_{32} & a_{33} & a_{34} \\ k_4 & a_{42} & a_{43} & a_{44} \end{vmatrix}}{\begin{vmatrix} a_{11} & a_{12} & a_{13} & a_{14} \\ a_{21} & a_{22} & a_{23} & a_{24} \\ a_{31} & a_{32} & a_{33} & a_{34} \\ a_{41} & a_{42} & a_{43} & a_{44} \end{vmatrix}}$$

$$x_2 = \frac{\begin{vmatrix} a_{11} & k_1 & a_{13} & a_{14} \\ a_{21} & k_2 & a_{23} & a_{24} \\ a_{31} & k_3 & a_{33} & a_{34} \\ a_{41} & k_4 & a_{43} & a_{44} \end{vmatrix}}{\begin{vmatrix} a_{11} & a_{12} & a_{13} & a_{14} \\ a_{21} & a_{22} & a_{23} & a_{24} \\ a_{31} & a_{32} & a_{33} & a_{34} \\ a_{41} & a_{42} & a_{43} & a_{44} \end{vmatrix}}$$

$$x_3 = \frac{\begin{vmatrix} a_{11} & a_{12} & k_1 & a_{14} \\ a_{21} & a_{22} & k_2 & a_{24} \\ a_{31} & a_{32} & k_3 & a_{34} \\ a_{41} & a_{42} & k_4 & a_{44} \end{vmatrix}}{\begin{vmatrix} a_{11} & a_{12} & a_{13} & a_{14} \\ a_{21} & a_{22} & a_{23} & a_{24} \\ a_{31} & a_{32} & a_{33} & a_{34} \\ a_{41} & a_{42} & a_{43} & a_{44} \end{vmatrix}}$$

$$x_4 = \frac{\begin{vmatrix} a_{11} & a_{12} & a_{13} & k_1 \\ a_{21} & a_{22} & a_{23} & k_2 \\ a_{31} & a_{32} & a_{33} & k_3 \\ a_{41} & a_{42} & a_{43} & k_4 \end{vmatrix}}{\begin{vmatrix} a_{11} & a_{12} & a_{13} & a_{14} \\ a_{21} & a_{22} & a_{23} & a_{24} \\ a_{31} & a_{32} & a_{33} & a_{34} \\ a_{41} & a_{42} & a_{43} & a_{44} \end{vmatrix}}.$$

PROGRAMMING THE METHOD

The subroutine of the previous program which evaluates a determinant by condensation can be used in the denominator of each of the above quotients. It can be used directly to evaluate $|A|$; the numerators can be found by substituting the elements in the appropriate column of $|A|$ with the constants k. This is done at line 470 in the program solving simultaneous equations in Appendix 9.

The re-writing of the *BASIC* program in 'C' involved similar problems to those previously described for the matrix program and so will not be considered further here. The print out of the 'C' version for *Windows* computers is in Appendix 2, p. 115.

APPLICATION OF THE PROGRAM TO A PRACTICAL PROGRAM IN ENGINEERING SCIENCE

Consider the circuit in Fig. 4. Using equations (5) - (8) on p.53, the equations to be solved are:

$-(22 \times 33 + 10 \times 33 + 10 \times 22).v_2 + 10 \times 33.v_3 = -22 \times 33 \times 6$

$68 \times 4.8.v_2 - (68 \times 4.8 + 22 \times 4.8 + 22 \times 68).v_3 + 22 \times 4.8.v_4 = 0$

$100 \times 22.v_3 - (100 \times 220 + 68 \times 220 + 68 \times 100).v_4 + 68 \times 220.v_5 = 0$

$47 \times 440.v_4 - (100 \times 47 + 47.440 + 100.440).v_5 = -100 \times 47 \times 6.$

Simplifying and rearranging give:

$$-1276v_2 + 330v_3 \qquad\qquad\qquad = -4356$$
$$326.4v_2 - 1928v_3 + 105.6v_4 \qquad = 0$$
$$22000v_3 - 43760v_4 + 14960v_5 = 0$$
$$20680v_4 - 69380v_5 = -28200$$

.

Using the program,

```
Enter the number of unknowns   4

Enter the coefficient of u1 in row 1   -1276

Enter the coefficient of u2 in row 1   330

Enter the coefficient of u3 in row 1   0

Enter the coefficient of u4 in row 1   0

Enter the coefficient of u1 in row 2   326.4

Enter the coefficient of u2 in row 2   -1928

Enter the coefficient of u3 in row 2   105.6

Enter the coefficient of u4 in row 2   0

Enter the coefficient of u1 in row 3   0

Enter the coefficient of u2 in row 3   22000

Enter the coefficient of u3 in row 3   -43760

Enter the coefficient of u4 in row 3   14960

Enter the coefficient of u1 in row 4   0

Enter the coefficient of u2 in row 4   0

Enter the coefficient of u3 in row 4   20680

Enter the coefficient of u4 in row 4   -69380
Enter the constant (rhs) in row 1   -4356

Enter the constant (rhs) in row 2   0

Enter the constant (rhs) in row 3   0

Enter the constant (rhs) in row 4   -28200_
The equations to be solved are:

-1276u1 +330u2 +0u3 +0u4 = -4356
326.4u1 -1928u2 +105.6u3 +0u4 = 0
0u1 +22000u2 -43760u3 +14960u4 = 0
0u1 +0u2 +20680u3 -69380u4 = -28200
```

```
Press any key to continue

u1=3.577648 u2=0.633577 u3=0.509385 u4=0.558289
Check by substituting the solutions in the equations (press any key)

The constants (right hand sides) are:

-4355.999512
-0.000311
0.001614
-28199.998047
```

the solution (quoted to 2 s.f.) is therefore:

$v_2 = 3.6$ volt $\qquad\qquad v_4 = 0.51$ volt

$v_3 = 0.63$ volt $\qquad\qquad v_5 = 0.56$ volt.

Given the voltage values, the current in any resistor can, of course, be found by Ohm's law using the voltage difference between the terminals of the resistor. For example, the current in R_3 is:

$$\frac{v_3 - v_4}{R_3} = \frac{0.63 - 0.51}{68} = 1.8 \text{ mA}$$

Note that since v_1 is known, v_2 is represented in the program by u_1, v_3 by u_2, v_4 by u_3 and v_5 by u_4.

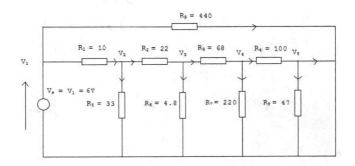

FIG. 4 : A CIRCUIT CONTAINING RESISTANCES AND A VOLTAGE SOURCE

3. THE DEVELOPMENT OF A COMPUTER PROGRAM TO SOLVE POLYNOMIAL EQUATIONS FOR USE IN ENGINEERING SCIENCE APPLICATIONS

INTRODUCTION

THE TRANSFER CHARACTERISTIC OF A D.C. AMPLIFIER

Consider the transfer (input-output) characteristic if a D.C. amplifier shown in Fig. 5. This can be represented by a power series of the type:

$$v_0 = a + bv + cv^2 + dv^3 + ev^4 + ...,$$

where v_0 is the output voltage and v the input voltage. This equation can be rearranged to be in the form of the polynomial equation $f(x) = 0$ where

$$f(x) = \text{constant} + a_1x + a_2x^2 + a_3x^3 + a_4x^4 + ...$$

with constant $= (a - v_0)$, $a_1 = b$, $a_2 = c$, $a_3 = d$ and $a_4 = e$.

The question arises, given appropriate values of the coefficients of v^n, what is the minimum value of input voltage v which will produce a given output voltage v_0?

68

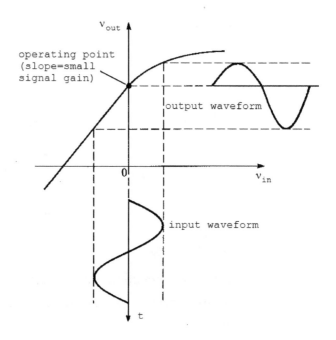

FIG 5 : THE TRANSFER CHARACTERISTIC OF
A D.C. AMPLIFIER

SOLVING POLYNOMIAL EQUATIONS

Since there are no formulae for higher-order polynomial equations, iterative approximation methods have to be resorted to solve these equations.

A METHOD OF SOLVING POLYNOMIAL EQUATIONS USING THE NEWTON-RAPHSON APPROACH

Suppose that the polynomial equation $y = f(x)$ has a an initial approximate solution (i.e. for which $f(x) = 0$) of $x = a$, a second approximation is equal to:

$a - f(a)/f'(a)$.

If this process is repeated, closer and closer approximations to a solution can be obtained. This is the essence of the Newton Raphson method.

In the case of polynomials, finding $f'(x)$ is straight forward because every term in a polynomial $f(x)$ is of the form $a_k x^k$, the first derivative of which is simply $a_k.k.x^{k-1}$, and differentiating a polynomial of order n therefore gives rise to another polynomial of order n - 1.

PROGRAMMING THE METHOD

A polynomial equation can have real solutions only, complex solutions only, or a combination of real and complex solutions. Programming is simplified by in the first instance considering only real solutions to the polynomial equation or real 'roots' of the polynomial.

CALCULATING THE VALUE OF A POLYNOMIAL

Looking at equation (1) above, the first requirement of the program is for a subroutine which calculates the values of $f(x)$ and $f'(x)$ for a given value of x. This begins at line 780 in the printout in Appendix 10, which calculates $f(a)$ and $f'(a)$. The coefficient of a^i is in $a(i)$ and at exit from the subroutine the calculated value of the polynomial with $x = a$ is in p.

FINDING THE FIRST ROOT OF THE POLYNOMIAL

A subroutine which finds f'(x) is at line 640, and it is evaluated at a using the subroutine at line 780.

Line 550 calculates each successive approximation

a - f(a)/f'(a),

with f(a) in yr and f'(a) in y1r (the expression at line 550 provides for complex roots which are discussed later).

If the difference between successive approximations is <0.0000001 (line 280), this is taken as a solution.

FINDING SUBSEQUENT SOLUTIONS

Having found one solution, the problem arises of how to find the others. Repeating the iteration procedure with the same polynomial would just lead to the same solution being found. The answer to the problem is to 'take out' the previously found root of the inputted polynomial by dividing it through by (x - a), where a is the previously found root.

Suppose a, a', a'', a''', a^{iv}, ... are

the roots of $f_n(x)=0$. Then

$$f(x) = a_n(x - a)(x - a')(x - a'')(x - a''')(x - a^{iv})...$$

Dividing the r.h.s. through by (x - a) gives

$$f_{n-1}(x) = a_n(x - a')(x - a'')(x - a''')(x - a^{iv})...$$

and so a is no longer a root (unless it is a repeated root) and if the iterative procedure is repeated with $f_{n-1}(x)$ a new root will be found (given that equation (1) converges).

The number of iterations is set to a maximum of 300 (line 500), and if successive approximations do not converge such that the difference between them is 0.000001, "No root found" is printed out and execution of the program stops. The maximum number of iterations can, of course, be increased if required.

INITIAL VALUE OF THE APPROXIMATION

It is not necessary to start with a value of a which is close to one solution of $f(x) = 0$. In practice, an initial setting of $a = 1$ worked satisfactorily.

FINDING COMPLEX SOLUTIONS

Having succeeded in producing a program which finds the solutions to polynomial equations having real solutions only, the final step in developing the program is to extend it to polynomial equations having complex solutions.

COMPLEX CONJUGATE ROOTS

Since the coefficient a_i of x^i are real, complex roots come in 'conjugate pairs'. Thus, if $a = b + ic$ is a root, then so is $b - ic$.

EXTENDING THE SUBROUTINE TO TO FIND a - f(a)/f'(a) FOR COMPLEX NUMBERS

To find complex roots, the first approximation must be a complex number and in practice, after some trial and error, setting this to $1 + 0.99i$ was found to work satisfactorily, in that it enabled complex solutions to most polynomial equations to be found.

Since a is now a complex number, generally the expression in equation (1) above has the form:

$$a - f(a)/f'(a) = c + id - (e + if)/(g + ih),$$

where $a = c + id$, $f(a) = e + if$ and $f'(a) = g + ih$. This is equal to:

$$c + id - (e + if)(g - ih)/(g^2 + h^2)$$

$$= c + id - [(eg + fh)/(g^2 + h^2) + (fg - eh)/(g^2 + h^2)i]$$

$$= [c - eg + fh)/(g^2 + h^2)] + [d - fg - eh)/(g^2 + h^2)i]$$

   (i)   (ii).

With changes of variable, the real part of the expression in the R.H.S. (i) is in line 550 in Appendix 10 and the imaginary part (ii) in 560. This is the next approximation which is then stored in a and b in the program, replacing the previous approximations.

FINDING SUCCESSIVE COMPLEX SOLUTIONS

Having found a complex root of the inputted polynomial and therefore another which is its complex conjugate, the polynomial has to be divided by (x - [a + ib])(x - [a - ib]) after the manner described for real roots, so that, effectively, this root is taken out of the resulting quotient (i.e. the next lower order polynomial). The subroutine to do this is at line 930.

CHECKING THE SOLUTION

Line 400f., inserts each solution found by the program into the inputted polynomial equation and evaluates the result (which is then printed out), which should of course be zero or very near (allowing for the six s.f. accuracy built into the program- which is also easily changed if required).

THE 'C' VERSION OF THE PROGRAM

The subroutine function_1050 in Appendix 3 moves up each coefficient k_i of x^i one place in the array containing the coefficients of the next lower order polynomial which results from dividing through by the previously found root.

The re-writing of the BASIC program in 'C' involved similar problems to those previously described for the matrix program and so will not be considered further here. The print out of the 'C' version for running on *Windows* computers is in Appendix 3.

APPLICATION OF THE PROGRAM TO A PRACTICAL PROBLEM IN ENGINEERING SCIENCE

Referring back to the situation in Fig. 5, consider the 'push-pull' output stage in Fig. 6.

The two transistors shown are matched n-p-n and p-n-p types. A positive input signal switches T_1 to conduct, 'pushing' current into the load. A negative input signal causes T_2 to conduct, 'pulling' current through the load.

The transfer characteristic for T_1 is:

$i_1 = a + bv + cv^2 + dv^3 + ev^4 + fv^5...$, subsequent terms being negligible.

For T_2 it is:

$i_2 = a + b(-v) + c(-v)^2 + d(-v)^3 + e(-v)^4 + f(-v)^5 + ...$

The resulting load current i_L is therefore:

$i_L = i_1 - i_2 = 2bv + 2dv^3 + 2fv^5$, neglecting higher order terms, and $v_0 = V_L = i_L R_L$.

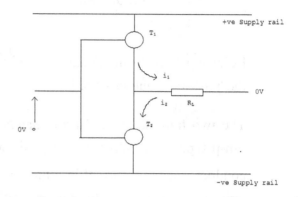

FIG 6: CIRCUIT DIAGRAM OF A PUSH-PULL
AMPLIFIER

Suppose that b = 10, d = 1 and f = 0.05 and that the maximum value of i_L required is 3A. If R_L is 15Ω, what is the minimum input voltage amplitude v given the maximum load current?

We have

$$V_L = v_0 = 3x15 = 20v + 2v^3 + 0.1v^5 .$$

Setting up the polynomial equation f(x) = 0 gives:

$$0 = -45 + 20v + 2v^3 + 0.1v^5 .$$

Entering the expression in the R.H.S. into the program:

```
The coefficient of x^2 is 12

The coefficient of x^1 is 8

and the constant is 1

Entering these values when prompted gives the solutions:

-0.156636, -0.534605 and -11.299858


Enter the order of the equation (i.e. highest power of x)  5

Enter the coefficient of x^5    .1

Enter the coefficient of x^4    0

Enter the coefficient of x^3    2

Enter the coefficient of x^2    0

Enter the coefficient of x^1    20

Enter the constant     -45_
Roots are (to 6 d.p.):

1.694065
-2.052780 +/-3.238155i
1.205747 +/-4.076397i

Inserting each root into f(x), f(x)=

0.000000 +0.000000i
0.000000 -0.000000i
0.000000 +0.000000i
-0.000000 +0.000000i
-0.000000 -0.000000i
```

The solutions (quoted to 3 s.f.) are;

$v = 1.69$ volt,

$v = -2.05 \pm 3.24j$ volt

$v = 1.21 \pm 4.08j$ volt.

Only real solutions are of interest here and so
v = 1.69 volt is the minimum input voltage which
produces a load current of 3A in a 15Ω load.

CONCLUSION

The development of three computer programs in *BASIC* and 'C' versions (for *Windows* computers) in solving practical problems in Engineering Science has been described.

The first is a program to invert matrices with complex elements which finds the inverted matrix by dividing the adjoint matrix of the inputted matrix by the value of its determinant. When used with a transmission matrix approach to solving A.C. circuits for currents and voltages, it provides a much less laborious method than using current and voltage laws. Although the program was illustrated with 2x2 matrices, the program can be used to invert higher-order matrices. In fact, the author has used it successfully to invert 10x10 matrices with complex elements.

The second program solves higher-order simultaneous equations. The mathematical approach on which the first program is based produces the solution set in the form of quotients, with the value of the determinant containing the coefficients of the unknowns in each equation as rows as divisor. The dividend is the same determinant only with the column of r.h.s. constants in the equations substituted for the corresponding column. In solving D.C. circuits, a fairly complex circuit of resistors and voltage source can give rise to 4 or more unknown voltages giving four or more equations in four or more unknowns to solve. The program comes up with the required solution voltages once the required coefficient of each unknown voltage is calculated from the circuit resistance values.

The third program solves polynomial equations of the form $0 = constant + a_1x + a_2x^2 + a_3x^3 + a_4x^4 + ...$ using an iterative, successive approximation approach based on Newton-Raphson's method and is especially useful with higher order polynomial equations, for which formulae are either complex or non-existent. The program was applied to the transfer characteristics of a push-pull amplifier output stage to find a minimum voltage which would produce the required load current. When the polynomial equation has complex solutions, the program finds these also (in most cases).

90

APPENDICES

APPENDIX 1: PRINT-OUT OF OF THE MATRIX INVERSION PROGRAM IN C

/*INVERTS A MATRIX [a] CONTAINING COMPLEX ELEMENTS USING inv [a]= adjoint [a]/det [a] */

/*Written by P. Trigger*/

```
#include <conio.h>
#include <stdio.h>
#include <math.h>
#define PI 3.141593
int e,f,g,h,m,n,o,q,s,t,v,y,i,j,k,l; /*n=order of matrix*/
```

float r,th,ee,ff,a[20][20],b[20][20],x[20][20],z[20][20],inv1[20][20],inv2[20][20];/*a?[][] is input matrix, inv?[][] its inverse*/

float

```
a1[20][20],a2[20][20],z1[20][20],z2[20][20],y1[2][
2],y2[2][2],x1[20][20],x2[20][20];

float
xx,zz,a3[2][2],a4[2][2],d1[2][2],d2[2][2],b1[20][20
],b2[20][20],x3[20][20],x4[20][20],aa,bb,cc,dd;

float in_float(void);
int in_int(void);
void evaluate_determinant(void);
void swop_rows(void);
void put_x_in_a(void);
void flush_array(void);
void multiply_matrices(void);

void evaluate_determinant_divisor(void);
void _elemult(void);
void _kthroot(void);

main()
        {
        cprintf("Written by P. Trigger\r\n\n\n");
        cprintf("An example in the use of the
program\r\n\n\n");
        cprintf("Consider the matrix:\r\n\n\n");
        cprintf("1+2j   3+4j\r\n\n");
        cprintf("5+6j   7+8j\r\n\n");
```

```
        cprintf("The order of the matrix to be
inverted is 2\r\n\n");
        cprintf("The REAL part of the element in
row 1 column 1 is 1, imaginary part 2\r\n\n");
        cprintf("The REAL part of the element in
row 1 column 2 is 3, imaginary part 4\r\n\n");
        cprintf("The REAL part of the element in
row 2 column 1 is 5, imaginary part 6\r\n\n");
        cprintf("The REAL part of the element in
row 2 column 2 is 8, imaginary part 2\r\n\n");
        cprintf("Entering these values when
prompted gives the inverted matrix:\r\n\n\n");
        cprintf("-0.5+0.4375j   0.25-0.1875j\r\n\n");
        cprintf("0.375-0.3125j   -0.125
+0.0625j\r\n\n");


        /*INPUT MATRIX */
        cprintf("Enter the order of the matrix to be
inverted");
        n=in_int();

        for (i=1;i<=n;i++)
                {
                for (j=1;j<=n;j++)
                        {
                        cprintf("\r\n\nEnter the
```

REAL part of the element in row %i column %i\r\n",i,j);

```
a1[i][j]=in_float();
z1[i][j]=a1[i][j];
```

cprintf("\r\n\nEnter the IMAGINARY part of the element in row %i column %i\r\n",i,j);

```
a2[i][j]=in_float();
z2[i][j]=a2[i][j];
```

/*Z?[][] stores input matrix */

```
        }
    }
```

/*PRINT OUT THE INPUT MATRIX*/

```
        clrscr();
        cprintf("The matrix [a] to be
inverted is;\r\n\n");
    for (i=1;i<=n;i++)
        {
        for (j=1;j<=n;j++)
            {
            cprintf("%f j%f
",z1[i][j],z2[i][j]);
```

```
                              }

                    cprintf("\r\n");
             }

getch();

evaluate_determinant();


d1[1][1]=x1[1][1],d2[1][1]=x2[1][1]; /*d?[][] is
value of determinant of input matrix*/


/*Calculate elements (determinants) of adjoint of
[a]*/

for (e=1;e<=n;e++)
       {
       for (f=1;f<=n;f++)
              {
              for (g=1;g<=n-1;g++)
                     {
                     q=g;
                     for (h=1;h<=n-1;h++)
                            {
```

```
                    y=h;
                    if (h>=f)
                        {
                        y=h+1;
                        }
                    if (g>=e)
                            {
                            q=g+1;
                            }
/*Build co-factor (determinant) of [a] element
(e,f)*/


                    a1[g][h]=z1[q][y];
                    a2[g][h]=z2[q][y];


                        }


                }
        if (n==2)
            {
            x1[1][1]=a1[g-1][h-1];
            x2[1][1]=a2[g-1][h-1];
            goto cont1;
            }



            n=g-1;
```

```
                evaluate_determinant();

                n=g;
                cont1: /*transpose elements
and assign proper sign*/
                /*divide by det [a] to
give inv [a](f,e)*/


                inv1[f][e]=pow(-
1,(e+f))*((x1[1][1]*d1[1][1]+x2[1][1]*d2[1][1])/(d
1[1][1]*d1[1][1]+d2[1][1]*d2[1][1]));
inv2[f][e]=pow(-1,(e+f))*((x2[1][1]*d1[1][1]-
x1[1][1]*d2[1][1])/(d1[1][1]*d1[1][1]+d2[1][1]*d2
[1][1]));



                }
        }
        clrscr();
        cprintf("Inverted matrix is;\r\n\n");
        for (i=1;i<=n;i++)
                {
                for (j=1;j<=n;j++)
                        {
                        cprintf("%f j%f
```

```
",inv1[i][j],inv2[i][j]);
                }
        cprintf("\r\n");
        }




cprintf("\r\n\nCheck by calculating product of input
matrix and its calculated inverse\r\n");
getch();

for (i=1;i<=n;i++)
        {
        for (j=1;j<=n;j++)
                {
                a[i][j]=inv1[i][j];
                b[i][j]=z1[i][j];
                }
        }

flush_array();
multiply_matrices();

for (i=1;i<=n;i++)
        {
        for (j=1;j<=n;j++)
                {
```

```
                        b2[i][j]=b1[i][j];
                        a[i][j]=inv2[i][j];
                        }
                }

flush_array();
multiply_matrices();

for (i=1;i<=n;i++)
        {
        for (j=1;j<=n;j++)
                {
                a1[i][j]=b1[i][j];
                a[i][j]=inv1[i][j];
                }
        }




for (i=1;i<=n;i++)
        {
        for (j=1;j<=n;j++)
                {
                b[i][j]=z2[i][j];


                }
        }
```

```
flush_array();
multiply_matrices();

for (i=1;i<=n;i++)
        {
        for (j=1;j<=n;j++)
                {
                a2[i][j]=b1[i][j];
                a[i][j]=inv2[i][j];
                }
        }

flush_array();
multiply_matrices();

for (i=1;i<=n;i++)
        {
        for (j=1;j<=n;j++)
                {
                x4[i][j]=b1[i][j];
                }
        }

for (i=1;i<=n;i++)
        {
        for (j=1;j<=n;j++)
```

```
                {
cprintf("%f j%f ",b2[i][j]-x4[i][j],a1[i][j]+a2[i][j]);
                }
        cprintf("\r\n");
          }
getch();
exit(1);



}
/*MAIN ENDS*/


/*
 *function evaluate_determinant()
 *================================
 */


void evaluate_determinant (void)
        {
        xx=1;/*initialize re and im signs of det
multiplier*/
        zz=1;
        cprintf("\r\n");

        for (k=n-1;k>=1;k--)  /*CONDENSE
DETERMINANT ORDER n to n-1,n-2...1*/
```

```
{


    swop_rows();


        for (i=1;i<=k;i++)/*Calculate
elements of determinant*/
            {
            for (j=1;j<=k;j++)
                {
        /*Hold elements of condensed
determinant*/

x1[i][j]=a1[1][1]*a1[i+1][j+1]-
a2[1][1]*a2[i+1][j+1]-
a1[i+1][1]*a1[1][j+1]+a2[i+1][1]*a2[1][j+1];

x2[i][j]=a2[1][1]*a1[i+1][j+1]+a2[i+1][j+1]*a1[1][
1]-a2[i+1][1]*a1[1][j+1]-a2[1][j+1]*a1[i+1][1];
                }
            }
        y1[1][1]=1;/*initialize re im
det multiplier*/
        y2[1][1]=0;
        if (k>1)
            {
```

```
        evaluate_determinant_divisor();
                    }


        put_x_in_a(); /*Put next lowest
order determinant back in a?[][]*/
                }
        x1[1][1]=xx*x1[1][1];/*sign of multiplier
re,im*/
        x2[1][1]=zz*x2[1][1];
        return(1);


        }




/* function put_x_in_a()
 *========================
 * puts x?[][] in a?[][]
 */

void put_x_in_a(void)
        {
        for (i=1;i<=k;i++)
```

```
            {
    for (j=1;j<=k;j++)
            {
            if(k>1)
                    {
                    _elemult();
                    }
            a1[i][j]=x1[i][j];
            a2[i][j]=x2[i][j];


            }
        }


    }
```

```
/*
 * function in_int()
 * ====================
 * inputs an integer number from the keyboard
 */



int in_int(void)
```

```
        {
        char tbuff[12];
        int d;
        tbuff[0] = 10;
        cgets(tbuff);
        sscanf(&tbuff[2],"%i",&d);
        return(d);
        }
```

```
/*
 * end of in_int()
 */
```

```
/*
 * function in_float()
 * ====================
 * inputs a floating-point number from the
keyboard
 */
```

```
float in_float(void)
        {
```

```
char tbuff[12];
float d;
tbuff[0] = 10;
cgets(tbuff);
sscanf(&tbuff[2],"%f",&d);
return(d);
}
```

```
/*
 * end of in_float()
 */
```

```
/*
 * function swop_rows()
 * ====================
 * swops rows to obtain largest pivot
 */

void swop_rows(void)
    {
        for (m=1;m<=k;m++)
```

/*Swop rows for largest pivot a1[1][1]*/

```
{
clrscr();
if
((fabs(a1[1][1]))>(fabs(a1[1+m][1])))
{
goto cont1;
}
xx=xx*-1;
zz=zz*-1;
/*If swopped change
determinant sign*/
for
(o=1;o<=k+1;o++)
{

clrscr();

b1[1][o]=a1[1][o];

b2[1][o]=a2[1][o];

a1[1][o]=a1[1+m][o];

a2[1][o]=a2[1+m][o];

a1[1+m][o]=b1[1][o];
```

```
                a2[1+m][o]=b2[1][o];
                                                    }
                            cont1:
                            clrscr();
                    }
                }

/*
 * function evaluate_determinant_divisor
 *
====================================
====
 * calculates pivot^(k-1)
 */

void evaluate_determinant_divisor(void)
            {
            aa=a1[1][1],bb=a2[1][1];
            a3[1][1]=1,a4[1][1]=0;

            for(l=1;l<=k-1;l++)
                {
                cc=a3[1][1],dd=a4[1][1];
                a3[1][1]=cc*aa-dd*bb;
                a4[1][1]=dd*aa+cc*bb;
                }
```

```
        aa=y1[1][1];
        /*Calculate determinant multiplier
(y1[1][1]+jy2[1][1])/(a?[][]^(k-1))*/



y1[1][1]=a3[1][1]/(a3[1][1]*a3[1][1]+a4[1][1]*a4[
1][1]);
        y2[1][1]=-
a4[1][1]/(a3[1][1]*a3[1][1]+a4[1][1]*a4[1][1]);
        _kthroot();
        return(1);

        }

/*
 * function flush_array
 * =====================
 * flushes b1[][]
 */

void flush_array(void)
        {
        for (i=1;i<=n;i++)
                {
                for (j=1;j<=n;j++)
```

```
                          {
                          b1[i][j]=0;
                          }
                     }
                }


/*
 * function multiply_matrices
 * ==========================
 * multiplies two matrices
 */

void multiply_matrices(void)
          {
          for (k=1;k<=n;k++)
               {
               for (i=1;i<=n;i++)
                    {
                    for (j=1;j<=n;j++)
                         {

     b1[i][k]=b1[i][k]+a[i][j]*b[j][k];
                         }
                    }
               }
          }
```

```c
/*
 * function _elemult()
 * ====================
 * multiplies elements by element multiplier
 */
void _elemult(void)
        {
        aa=x1[i][j];
        x1[i][j]=x1[i][j]*y1[1][1]-x2[i][j]*y2[1][1];
        x2[i][j]=x2[i][j]*y1[1][1]+y2[1][1]*aa;
        return(1);
        }
/*
 * end of _elemult()
 */
```

```
/*
 * function _kthroot()
 * ====================
 * finds kth root of determinant multiplier giving
element multiplier, re im
 */
void _kthroot(void)
        {

r=sqrt(y1[1][1]*y1[1][1]+y2[1][1]*y2[1][1]);/*mag
nitude*/
        if(y1[1][1]<0)
                {
                y2[1][1]=y2[1][1]*-1;/*multiply im
by -1*/
                }
        if(fabs(y1[1][1]/r)<0.0000001)
                {
                th=PI/(2*k);
                goto cont12;
                }

        th=y1[1][1]/r;/*arg=th*/
        th=sqrt(1-th*th)/th;
        th=atan(th)/k;
```

```
cont12:        aa=pow(r,(double)1/k)*cos(th);

        if(fabs(y2[1][1]/r)>0.9999999)
                {

        th=PI/(2*k)*(y2[1][1]/fabs(y2[1][1]));
                goto cont13;
                }

        th=y2[1][1]/r;
        th=th/sqrt(1-th*th);
        th=atan(th)/k;

cont13:        bb=pow(r,(double)1/k)*sin(th);
        if(y1[1][1]>=0)
                {
                goto cont10;
                }
        cc=cos(PI/(double)k);/*re is -ve so multiply
re,im by (-1)^(1/k)*/
        dd=sin(PI/(double)k);
        ee=cc*aa-dd*bb;
        ff=dd*aa+bb*cc;
        y1[1][1]=ee;
        y2[1][1]=ff;
```

```
        goto cont11;
cont10:      y1[1][1]=aa;
        y2[1][1]=bb;


cont11:      return(1);
        }




/*
 * end of _kthroot()
 */

/*PROGRAM ENDS*/
```

APPENDIX 2: PRINT-OUT OF THE SIMULTANEOUS EQUATION-SOLVING PROGRAM IN C

```
/*SOLVES SIMULTANEOUS EQUATIONS BY
EVALUATING THE DETERMINANT OF
COEFFICIENTS (divisor), */
/*THE DETERMINANT OF COEFFICIENTS
WITH SUBSTITUTED CONSTANTS (dividend)
AND THEN DIVIDING*/

/*Written by P. Trigger*/

#include <conio.h>
#include <stdio.h>
#include <math.h>

int m,n,o,s,t,i,i1,j,j1,k,d1[20][20],d2[20][1];
/*n=order of equations*/

float u[20][1],p[20][1],l[20][1],y,x1,d; /*l[][]
contains rhs constants*/
float a[20][20],b[20][20],x[20][20],z[20][20];

float in_float(void);
int in_int(void);
```

```
void evaluate_determinant(void);
void swop_rows(void);
void put_x_in_a(void);
void put_z_in_a(void);




main()
     {
     cprintf("Program written by P.
Trigger\r\n\n\n");
     cprintf("Equations to be solved must be in
the form:\r\n\n"
          "a.u1 + b.u2 + c.u3 + d.u4 + .... +
k.un = a constant\r\n\n"
          "where u1, u2, u3,..., un are the
unknowns; a, b, c,....,k their coefficients\r\n\n");



     cprintf("\r\n\nEXAMPLE:\r\n\n");
     cprintf(" 4x -2y = 8    (row 1)\r\n");
     cprintf("-3x + 5y= -9.5  (row 2)\r\n\n");
     cprintf("Here, u1 is x, u2 is y. The
coefficient of u1 in row 1 is 4;\r\n");
     cprintf("the coefficient of u2 in row 1 is -2.
The constant in row 2 is -9.5");
```

```c
        cprintf("\r\n\nThe number of unknowns is
entered first, then all their coefficients,");
        cprintf("\r\nfollowed by all the constants
('right hand sides' (rhs)):\r\n");




/*INPUT MATRIX OF COEFFICIENTS OF
UNKNOWNS*/
        cprintf("\r\n\n\nEnter the number of
unknowns  ");
        n=in_int();


        for (i=1;i<=n;i++)
                {
                for (j=1;j<=n;j++)
                        {
                        cprintf("\r\n\nEnter the
coefficient of u%i in row %i  ",j,i);
                        a[i][j]=in_float();
                        d1[i][j]=j1; /*PRECISION
IN D.P.*/

                        z[i][j]=a[i][j];


                        }
                }
```

```
/*INPUT MATRIX OF RHS CONSTANTS*/
        for (i=1;i<=n;i++)
                {
        cprintf("\r\n\nEnter the constant
(rhs) in row %i   ",i);
                l[i][1]=in_float();
                d2[i][1]=j1; /*PRECISION IN
D.P.*/
                }


/*PRINT OUT THE EQUATIONS, append '+'
where appropriate*/
                clrscr();
                cprintf("The equations to be solved
are:\r\n\n");
        for (i=1;i<=n;i++)
                {
                for (j=1;j<=n;j++)
                        {
                        if (j!=1)
                                {
                                cprintf("%+.*fu%i
",d1[i][j],z[i][j],j);

                                goto cont3;
                                }
                        cprintf("%.*fu%i
```

```
",d1[i][j],z[i][j],j);
                cont3:  ;
                    }


                  cprintf("=
%.*f",d2[i][1],l[i][1]);
                    cprintf("\r\n");
                }
cprintf("\r\n\nPress any key to continue");

getch();
gotoxy(1,wherey());


        evaluate_determinant();
        d=x[1][1];




        put_z_in_a();



        for (t=1;t<=n;t++)
            {
```

```
            for (s=1;s<=n;s++)
                {
                a[s][t]=l[s][1];


                }
            y=1;
            evaluate_determinant();




            u[t][1]=x[1][1][1]/d;

            put_z_in_a();



                }

    for (j=1;j<=n;j++)
        {
        cprintf("u%i=%f ",j,u[j][1]);
        }



    cprintf("\r\nCheck by substituting the solutions in
    the equations (press any key)");
    getch();
```

```
gotoxy(1,wherey());
cprintf("");

                                        gotoxy
(1,wherey());
cprintf("\r\nThe constants (right hand sides)
are:\r\n\n");
        for (i=1;i<=n;i++)
                {
                for (j=1;j<=n;j++)
                        {

        p[i][1]=p[i][1]+z[i][j]*u[j][1];
                        }
                cprintf("%f",p[i][1]);
                cprintf("\r\n");
                }

getch();



        }


/*
*function evaluate_determinant()
*================================
*/
```

```
void evaluate_determinant (void)
    {
    x1=1;
    cprintf("\r\n");

    for (k=n-1;k>=1;k--)  /*CONDENSE
DETERMINANT ORDER n to n-1,n-2...1*/
        {


        swop_rows();


            for (i=1;i<=k;i++)/*Calculate
elements of determinant*/
                {
                for (j=1;j<=k;j++)
                    {

    x[i][j]=a[1][1]*a[i+1][j+1]-
a[i+1][1]*a[1][j+1];

                    }
                }

            put_x_in_a(); /*Put next lowest
order determinant back in a[][]*/
```

```
        }
    x[1][1]=x[1][1]*x1;


    }
```

```
/* function put_x_in_a[][]
 *=========================
 * puts x[][] in a[][]
 */

void put_x_in_a(void)
        {
        y=1/pow(a[1][1],k-1);
        x1=x1*y/fabs(y);

        for (i=1;i<=k;i++)
                {
```

```
for (j=1;j<=k;j++)
    {
    if(k>1)
        {

x[i][j]=x[i][j]*pow(fabs(y),(double)1/k);

        }
    a[i][j]=x[i][j];

    }
}

}
```

```
/* function put_z_in_a()
 * puts z[][] in a[][]
 */

void put_z_in_a(void)
    {
    for (i=1;i<=n;i++)
        {
        for (j=1;j<=n;j++)
```

```
                    {
                    a[i][j]=z[i][j];



                    }
                 }
              }
```

```
/*
 * function swop_rows()
 * ===================
 * swops rows to obtain largest pivot
 */


void swop_rows(void)
              {
                    for (m=1;m<=k;m++)
/*Swop rows for largest pivot a[1][1]*/
                    {
                    clrscr();
```

```
                    if
((fabs(a[1][1]))>(fabs(a[1+m][1])))
                            {
                            goto cont1;
                            }
                            x1=x1*-1;  /*If
swopped change determinant sign*/
                                for
(o=1;o<=k+1;o++)
                                    {

        clrscr();

        b[1][o]=a[1][o];

        a[1][o]=a[1+m][o];

        a[1+m][o]=b[1][o];
                                    }
                            cont1:
                            clrscr();
                        }
                    }


/*
 * function in_int()
```

```
 * ====================
 * inputs an integer number from the keyboard
 */


int in_int(void)
        {
        char tbuff[12];
        int d;
        tbuff[0] = 10;
        cgets(tbuff);
        sscanf(&tbuff[2],"%i",&d);
        return(d);
        }
/*
 * end of in_int()
 */



/*
 * function in_float()
 * ====================
 * inputs a floating-point number from the
keyboard
 */
```

```c
float in_float()
    {

        int i1;
        char tbuff[12];
        float d;
        tbuff[0] = 10;
        cgets(tbuff);
        sscanf(&tbuff[2],"%f",&d);

        for (i1=2;i1<=tbuff[1];i1++)
/*DETERMINE HOW MANY D.P, STORE THIS
IN j1*/
            {
            if (tbuff[i1]=='.')
                {
                j1=tbuff[1]-i1+1;
                goto cont2;
                }
            }
        j1=0;



cont2:  return(d);
        }
/*
 * end of in_float()
```

*/

130

APPENDIX 3: PRINT-OUT OF THE POLYNOMIAL EQUATION-SOLVING PROGRAM IN C

```c
#include <conio.h>
#include <stdio.h>
#include <math.h>

int n,n1,i,j,h,ii,jj,m,kk,l;

double _480(void);
double _780(void);
double _600(void);
double _920(void);
double _1050(void);
double in_float(void);
int in_int(void);

double
n2[50],aa[50],nn1[50],nn2[50],c[50],b1[3],r[50],r1[
50],a,b,p,q,yr,y1r,yi,y1i,a2,b2,f,e,k,bb[3],x;

main()
    {
    cprintf("Solves an equation f(x)=0, where
f(x) is a sum of terms in ascending powers of
x\r\n\n"

    "Program written by P. Trigger\r\n\n");

    cprintf("Example x^3 + 12x^2 + 8x + 1 =
```

0\r\n\n");
        cprintf("The order of the polynomial is
3\r\n\n");

        cprintf("The coefficient of x^3 is 1\r\n\n");
        cprintf("The coefficient of x^2 is 12\r\n\n");
        cprintf("The coefficient of x^1 is 8\r\n\n");
        cprintf("and the constant is 1\r\n\n");
        cprintf("Entering these values when
prompted gives the solutions:\r\n\n");
cprintf("-0.156636, -0.534605 and
-11.299858\r\n\n\n\n");
        cprintf("Enter the order of the equation (i.e.
highest power of x) ");
        n=in_int();

        n1=n;

        cont6:
        for (i=n+1;i>=2;i--)
                {
                cprintf("\r\n\nEnter the coefficient of
x^%i   ",i-1);
                aa[i]=in_float();
                if (aa[n+1]==0)
                        {
                        goto cont6;

```
                    }

            nn1[i]=aa[i];
            nn2[i]=aa[i];
            }
    cprintf("\r\n\nEnter the constant    ");
            aa[1]=in_float();
            nn1[1]=aa[1];
            nn2[1]=aa[1];
    cprintf("\r\n\nRoots are (to 6 d.p.):\r\n");

    for (h=1;h<=n1;h++)
            {
    _480();/*Find approximation to root
x(n+1)=x(n)-f(x)/f'(x)*/

            if (fabs(a)<0.0000001)
                    {
                    a=0;
                    }

            if (fabs(b)<0.0000001)
                    {
                    b=0;
                    cprintf("\r\n%lf",a);
                    r[ii]=a;
                    ii=ii+1;
```

```
                    jj=jj+1;
                    goto cont1;
                    }

          r[ii]=a;
          ii=ii+1;
          r[ii]=a;
          ii=ii+1;
          r1[jj]=b;
          jj=jj+1;
          r1[jj]=-b;
          jj=jj+1;
          cprintf("\r\n%lf +/-%lfi",a,fabs(b));
          if (fabs(b)>0) /*If root is imaginary,
find (x-root)(x-conjugate)*/
                    {
                    bb[3]=1;
                    bb[2]=-2*a;
                    bb[1]=a*a+b*b;
                    m=2;
                    goto cont2;
                    }

          cont1:
          m=1;
          bb[2]=1;
          bb[1]=-a;
```

```
                    cont2:
                    _920(); /*Divide by root or (x-
root)(x-conjugate)*/

                    if (m==2)
                            {
                            n=n-1;
                            h=h+1;
                            }
                    n=n-1;
                    }
cprintf("\r\n\nInserting each root into f(x),
f(x)=\r\n");
n=n1;
for (i=n+1;i>=1;i--)
        {
        aa[i]=nn2[i];
        nn1[i]=nn2[i];
        }
for (kk=0;kk<=n-1;kk++)
        {
        a=r[kk];
        b=r1[kk];

        _780();/*Evaluate f(x) using x=root*/
        cprintf("\r\n%lf %+lfi",p,q);
```

```
        }


getch();

        }



/*
 * function in_float()
 * ===================
 * inputs a floating-point number from the
keyboard
 */


double in_float(void)
        {
        char tbuff[12];
        double d;
        tbuff[0] = 10;
        cgets(tbuff);
        sscanf(&tbuff[2],"%lf",&d);
        return(d);
        }

/*
```

```
* end of in_float()
*/


/*
* function in_int()
* ====================
* inputs an integer number from the keyboard
*/


int in_int(void)
        {
        char tbuff[12];
        int d;
        tbuff[0] = 10;
        cgets(tbuff);
        sscanf(&tbuff[2],"%i",&d);
        return(d);
        }


/*
* end of in_int()
*/
```

```
/*
 * function _480()
 * ================
 * Finds closer approximation to root x(n+1)=x(n)-
f(x)/f'(x)
 */
double _480(void)
{
a=1; /*Initial values for re(x) and im(x)*/
b=1;

for (l=1;l<=500;l++)
        {
        _600();
        a2=a;
        b2=b;
        a=a-(yr*y1r+yi*y1i)/(y1r*y1r+y1i*y1i);
        b=b-(yi*y1r-yr*y1i)/(y1r*y1r+y1i*y1i);


        if (fabs(a2-a)<0.000000000001 &&
fabs(b2-b)<0.000000000001)
            /*If x(n+1)-x(n) is <1E-12, x(n)=root*/
                {
                return(1);
```

```
            }
        }

cprintf("\r\n\nNo root found");
exit(1);
return(1);
}

/*
 * end of _480()
 */

/*
 * function _600()
 * ================
 * Evaluates an f(x) and finds and evaluates f'(x)
 */
double _600(void)
{
_780();



yr=p;
yi=q;
```

```
for (i=n;i>=2;i--)/*Differentiate and put f'(x) in
aa[]*/
        {
        aa[i]=(double)i*nn1[i+1];
        }


aa[1]=nn1[2];
n=n-1;
_780();

if (p==0)/*Prevent f'(x)=0 in f(x)/f'(x)*/
        {
        p=0.1;
        }


y1r=p;
y1i=q;
n=n+1;

for (i=1;i<=n;i++)/*Put f(x) back in aa[]*/
        {
        aa[i]=nn1[i];
        }
return(1);
}
```

```
/*
 * end of _600()
 */

/*
 * _780()
 * ======
 * Evaluates a polynomial
 */
double _780(void)
{
e=1;
f=0;
p=0;
q=0;
for (i=n+1;i>=2;i--)
        {
        for (j=i;j>=2;j--)
                {
                k=e;
                e=e*a-f*b;
                f=f*a+k*b;
                }
```

```
        p=p+aa[i]*e;
        q=q+aa[i]*f;

        e=1;
        f=0;
        }
p=p+aa[1];/*Add in coefficient of x^0*/


return(1);

}

/*
 * end of _780()
 */


/*
 * function _920()
 * ==================
 * Divides one polynomial by another
 */
double _920(void)
{
for(i=n+1;i>=m;i--)
```

```
        {
        c[i-m]=aa[n+1]/bb[m+1];
        for (j=m+1;j>=1;j--)
                {
                aa[j+n-m]=aa[j+n-m]-c[i-m]*bb[j];
                }
        _1050();
        }

for (i=n-m+1;i>=1;i--)
        {
        aa[i]=c[i];
        nn1[i]=c[i];
        }

return (1);
}


/*
 * end of _920()
 */
```

```
/*
 * function _1050()
 * ==================
 * Shifts coefficients one place to left
 */
double _1050(void)
{
for (kk=n+1;kk>=2;kk--)
        {
        aa[kk]=aa[kk-1];
        }
return(1);
}
/*
 * end of _1050
 */
```

APPENDIX 4: COMPLEX MATRIX MULTIPLYING PROGRAM IN C

/*MULTIPLIES TWO MATRICES [a] [b] CONTAINING COMPLEX ELEMENTS USING*/
/*([a]re+j[a]im)([b]re+j[b]im)=[a]re.[b]re+j[a]im.[b]re+j[a]re.[b]im-[a]im.[b]im*/

/*Written by P. Trigger*/

```
#include <conio.h>
#include <stdio.h>
#include <math.h>

int c,d,e,f,n,r,s,i,j,k;
char g;
float
a1[20][20],a2[20][20],b[20][20],b1[20][20],b2[20][20],m1[20][20],m2[20][20],
x[20][20],x1[20][20],x2[20][20],x3[20][20],x4[20][20];
```

```
float in_float(void);
int in_int(void);
void set_x_zero(void);
void multiply_matrices(void);
void input_matrix(void);
void print_matrix(void);


main()
     {
     /*INPUT MATRICES */
     cprintf("\r\nEnter the number of rows of the
first matrix");
        r=in_int();

        cprintf("\r\nEnter the number of columns of
the first matrix");
        s=in_int();
        c=r,d=s;    /*Store number of rows and
columns*/


        input_matrix();

        for (i=1;i<=c;i++)
              {
              for (j=1;j<=d;j++)/*Put first matrix
```

in [a]*/

```
                    {
                    a1[i][j]=m1[i][j];   /*[a]re*/
                    a2[i][j]=m2[i][j];   /*[a]im*/

                    }
            }
```

cont1:
```
        cprintf("\r\nEnter the number of rows of the
second matrix");
        r=in_int();

        if(r!=d)
                {
                cprintf("\r\nNumber of rows in
second matrix must equal number of columns in
first matrix\r\n\n");
                goto cont1;
                }

        cprintf("\r\nEnter the number of columns of
the second matrix");
        s=in_int();
        e=r,f=s;
        input_matrix();
```

```
/*Put second matrix in [b]*/
    for (i=1;i<=e;i++)
                {
            for (j=1;j<=f;j++)
                {
                    b1[i][j]=m1[i][j];   /*[b]re*/
                    b2[i][j]=m2[i][j];   /*[b]im*/
                }
                }
```

```
            /*Store number of rows and
columns*/
```

```
    /*PRINT OUT INPUT MATRICES*/
    r=c,s=d;
    for (i=1;i<=r;i++)
            {
            for (j=1;j<=d;j++)/*Put first matrix
in [m1]*/
                {
                    m1[i][j]=a1[i][j];
                    m2[i][j]=a2[i][j];
```

```
                }
            }
        clrscr();
        cprintf("Matrix [a] is;\r\n\n");
        print_matrix();


        r=e,s=f;
        for (i=1;i<=r;i++)
            {
            for (j=1;j<=c;j++)/*Put second
matrix in [m1]*/
                {
                m1[i][j]=b1[i][j];
                m2[i][j]=b2[i][j];
                }
            }
        cprintf("\r\nMatrix [b] is;\r\n\n");
        print_matrix();

        /*Calculate [a]re.[b]re*/

        for (i=1;i<=c;i++)
            {
            for (j=1;j<=d;j++)
                {
                m1[i][j]=a1[i][j]; /*put a1[][]
in m1[][] for entry to multiply_matrices()*/
```

```
                                    }
                              }

            for (i=1;i<=e;i++)
                  {
                  for (j=1;j<=f;j++)
                        {
                        m2[i][j]=b1[i][j]; /* "   b1[][]
in m2[][] " */
                        }
                  }
            set_x_zero();          /*Reset x[][]*/
            r=c,s=f;
            multiply_matrices();
            for (i=1;i<=c;i++)
                  {
                  for (j=1;j<=f;j++)     /*Store in
x1[][]*/
                        {
                        x1[i][j]=x[i][j];
                        }
                  }

/*Calculate [a]im.[b]re*/

            for (i=1;i<=c;i++)
                  {
```

```
for (j=1;j<=d;j++)
    {
    m1[i][j]=a2[i][j];
    }
}


set_x_zero();          /*Reset x[][]*/
multiply_matrices();
for (i=1;i<=c;i++)
    {
    for (j=1;j<=f;j++)     /*Store in
x2[][]*/
            {
            x2[i][j]=x[i][j];
            }
    }

/*Calculate [a]re.[b]im*/

for (i=1;i<=c;i++)
    {
    for (j=1;j<=d;j++)
        {
        m1[i][j]=a1[i][j];
        }
    }
```

```
for (i=1;i<=e;i++)
        {
        for (j=1;j<=f;j++)
                {
                m2[i][j]=b2[i][j];
                }
        }
set_x_zero();           /*Reset x[][]*/
multiply_matrices();
for (i=1;i<=c;i++)
        {
        for (j=1;j<=f;j++)     /*Store in
x3[][]*/
                {
                x3[i][j]=x[i][j];
                }
        }


/*Calculate [a]im.[b]im*/

for (i=1;i<=c;i++)
        {
        for (j=1;j<=d;j++)
                {
                m1[i][j]=a2[i][j];
                }
```

```
        }


set_x_zero();           /*Reset x[][]*/
multiply_matrices();
for (i=1;i<=c;i++)
        {
        for (j=1;j<=f;j++)    /*Store in
x4[][]*/
                {
                x4[i][j]=x[i][j];
                }
        }
for (i=1;i<=c;i++)
        {
        for (j=1;j<=f;j++)
                {
                m1[i][j]=x1[i][j]-
x4[i][j],a1[i][j]=m1[i][j];

        m2[i][j]=x2[i][j]+x3[i][j];a2[i][j]=m2[i][j];
                d=f;
                }
        }
cprintf("\r\n\nProduct matrix is;\r\n\n");

print_matrix();
```

```
getch();
cprintf("\r\n\nMultiply result by another matrix
(y/n)?");

g=getch();
if (g!='y'&& g!='Y')
        {
        exit(1);
        }
        goto cont1;

}
/*MAIN ENDS*/

/*
 * function in_int()
 * ====================
 * inputs an integer number from the keyboard
 */


int in_int(void)
        {
        char tbuff[12];
        int d;
        tbuff[0] = 10;
```

```
        cgets(tbuff);
        sscanf(&tbuff[2],"%i",&d);
        return(d);
        }
```

```
/*
 * end of in_int()
 */
```

```
/*
 * function in_float()
 * ====================
 * inputs a floating-point number from the
keyboard
 */
```

```
float in_float(void)
        {
        char tbuff[12];
        float d;
        tbuff[0] = 10;
        cgets(tbuff);
        sscanf(&tbuff[2],"%f",&d);
```

```
        return(d);
        }

/*
 * end of in_float()
 */


/*
 * function set_x_zero()
 * =====================
 *
 */
void set_x_zero(void)
        {
        for (i=1;i<=r;i++)
                {
                for (j=1;j<=f;j++)
                        {
                        x[i][j]=0;
                        }
                }
        }
/*
 * end of set_x_zero()
 */

/*
```

```
 * function multiply_matrices
 * ===========================
 *
 */
void multiply_matrices(void)
        {
        for (k=1;k<=f;k++)
                {
                for (i=1;i<=c;i++)
                        {
                        for (j=1;j<=e;j++)
                                {

        x[i][k]=x[i][k]+m1[i][j]*m2[j][k];
                                }
                        }
                }
        }

/*
 * end of multiply_matrices()
 */

/*
 * function input_matrix()
 * ===========================
 *
```

```
*/
void input_matrix(void)
        {

for (i=1;i<=r;i++)
            {
            for (j=1;j<=s;j++)
                {
                cprintf("\r\n\nEnter element
in row %i column %i Real part\r\n",i,j);
                m1[i][j]=in_float();

                cprintf("\r\n\nEnter element
in row %i column %i Imaginary part\r\n",i,j);
                m2[i][j]=in_float();
                }
            }
        }
/*
 * end of input_matrix()
 */


/*
 * function print_matrix()
 * ===========================
 *
```

```
*/
void print_matrix(void)
{
for (i=1;i<=r;i++)
        {
        for (j=1;j<=s;j++)
                {
                cprintf("%f j%f  ",m1[i][j],m2[i][j]);
                }               cprintf("\r\n");
        }
}
/*
 * end of print_matrix()
 */
```

APPENDIX 5: *BASIC* SYNTAX USED

DIM variable name (number1,number2): dimensions a rectangular array of size number1 x number2.

variable name (number1,number2): contains the value of the element in the array variable name in row number1,column number2

INPUT variable name or variable name$: waits for a number or string to be keyed in, assigning the keyed-in value to variable name or variable name$

FOR variable name1=variable name2 or number to variable name3 or number: executes the code following the FOR instruction and ending in a NEXT variable name instruction variable name3 - variable name 2 times.

REM: is ignored by the program but is used for explanatory remarks

IF variable name1 logical operator variable name2 THEN instruction, where logical operator can be =, <, AND, etc: tests the truth of the operation. If true, the code following the THEN instruction is executed. If false, the code following the THEN instruction is ignored

GOSUB line number: executes the subroutine at line number. RETURN at the end of the subroutine returns control to the instruction following the GOSUB line number instruction

variable name1 or number1^variable name2 or number2: raises the value in variable name1 or number1 to the power variable name2 or number2

PRINT "characters" : prints out characters; PRINT variable name or variable name$ prints out the value of variable name or variable name$

ABS (expression): gives the absolute value of the expression

SQR expression: gives the square root of the value of the expression

COS and SIN (expression), with expression in radians: gives the cosine and sine of the value of expression

SGN (expression): gives the value -1 if expression is negative; 0 if expression is zero and 1 if expression is positive.

APPENDIX 6: 'C' SYNTAX USED

#INCLUDE<filename.h>: makes available routines for input and output and mathematical operations, etc

#DEFINE variable name number: sets the value of variable name to the value of number

INT variable name: declares variable name as an integer value

FLOAT variable name: declares variable name as a floating point value

variable name [number1,number2]:declares a rectangular array. Elements are integer values if the instruction is preceded by INT or floating point values if preceded by FLOAT

variable name [number]: declares a one-dimensional array
void subroutine name (void): declares a subroutine

subroutine name(); : executes the subroutine name
in_int and in_float: are standard keyboard input

subroutines

main(): declares the start of the main program

cprintf ("string"): prints out string;
cprintf("%f",variable name): prints out the floating
point value of variable name;
cprintf("\r\n"): executes a carriage return and
advances to the next line;
cprintf("variable name1.variable
name2%f",variable name3): prints out the value of
variable name3 to variable name2 d.p.

for (variable name1=variable name2 or
number1;variable name 1 to variable name3 or
number2;variable name1++): executes the
following code repeatedly whilst the centre
expression in the bracket is true-
for (variable name1=variable name2 or
number1;variable name 1 to variable name3 or
number2;variable name1++)
{
code
}

if (variable name1 logical expression variable
name2)

```
{
code
}
```

executes code repeatedly whilst the centre
expression in the brackets remains true

/*string*/ : is ignored by the compiler but serves
the purpose of explanation

pow (expression1,expression2): raises expression1
to the power expression2

clrscr: clears the screen
fabs(expression): gives the absolute value of
expression

sqrt variable name: gives the square root of the
value in variable name

(double) variable name: declares a floating point
number up to
$10^{+/-308}$

(float) variable name: declares a floating point
number up to
$10^{+/-37}$

sin (variable name) or cos (variable name): give the sine or cosine values of the angle variable name (in radians)

atn (variable name): gives the value of $\tan^{-1}$ (variable name)

goto cont number: passes control to the instruction beginning after the label cont number

goto (number,wherey()): resets the cursor to the line number, present column

APPENDIX 7: PRINT-OUT OF THE REAL MATRIX INVERSION PROGRAM IN *BASIC*

```
100 REM***Inverts a matrix [a] using inv [a]=adj
[a]/det [a]***

110 ?"Type in the matrix order"

120 input n:?

130 dim a(n,n):dim x(n,n)

140 dim y(n-1,n-1)

150 dim z(n,n):dim b(n,n):dim inv(n,n)

160 for i=1 to n

170 for j=1 to n

180 ?"input element in row";i;"column";j

190 input a(i,j)

200 REM *Hold input matrix*
```

210 z(i,j)=a(i,j)

220 next j:next i:?:?

230 ?"Matrix to be inverted is;"

240 for i=1 to n

250 for j=1 to n

260 ? z(i,j)

270 next j

280 ?

290 next i

300 ?

310 ?"Calculating..."

320 REM* d=value of determinant of input matrix *

330 gosub 630d=x(1,1)

340 REM*calculate elements of adj [a]*

350 for u=1 to n

360 for v=1 to n

370 for s=1 to n-1

380 x=s

390 for t=1 to n-1

400 y=t

410 if t>=v then y=t+1

420 if s>=u then x=s+1

430 REM*build cofactor of [a](u,v)*

440 a(s,t)=z(x,y)

450 next t

460 next s:if n=2 then x(1,1)=a(s-1,t-1):goto 510

470 REM*evaluate cofactor of [a](u,v) in x(1,1); transpose with proper

480 REM sign to give adj [a](v,u); divide by det [a] to give inv [a](v,u)

490 REM in inv(v,u)*

500 n=s-1:gosub 630:n=s

510 inv(v,u)=(-1)^(u+v)*x(1,1)/d

520 next v

530 next u

540 ?:?:?"Inverted matrix is;"

550 for i=1 to n

560 for j=1 to n

570 ? inv(i,j)

580 next j

590 ?

600 next i

610 ?:?gosub 950:stop

620 REM*calculates a det*

630 x=1

640 for k=n-1 to 1 step-1

650 gosub 830:if a(1,1)=0 then x(1,1)=0:return

660 REM*condense det [a] to next lowest order in x()*

670 for i=1 to k

680 for j=1 to k

690 x(i,j)=a(1,1)*a(i+1,j+1)-a(i+1,1)*a(1,j+1)

700 next j

710 next i

730 gosub 770

740 next k

750 x(1,1)=x*x(1,1)

755 return

760 REM*put det x() back into a()*

770 y=1/a(1,1)^(k-1):x=x*SGN(y)

775 for i=1 to k

780 for j=1 to k

785 if k>1then x(i,j)=x(i,j)*(SGN(y)*y)^(1/k)

790 a(i,j)=x(i,j)

800 next j

810 next i

820 return

830 for m=1 to k

840 REM*swop rows for largest a(?,1)*

850 IF ABS(a(1,1))>ABS(a(1+m,1)) then 930

860 REM*if rows swopped reverse determinant sign*

870 x=x*-1

880 for l=1 to k+1

890 b(1,1)=a(1,1)

900 a(1,1)=a(1+m,1)

910 a(1+m,1)=b(1,1)

920 next l

930 next m

940 return

950 REM*calculate product matrix of input matrix x inverse*

960 dim p(n,n)

970 for k=1 to n

980 for i=1 to n

990 for j=1 to n

1000 p(i,k)=p(i,k)+z(i,j)*inv(j,k)

1010 next j

1020 next i

1030 next k

1040 ?"Product of input and inverse matrix is;"

1050 for i=1 to n

1060 for j=1 to n

1070 ? p(i,j),

1080 next j

1090 ?

174

1100 next i

1110 ?

1120 return

APPENDIX 8: PRINT-OUT OF THE COMPLEX MATRIX INVERSION PROGRAM IN *BASIC*

```
100 REM FILE "cadjinv"***

110 REM****calculates the inverse of a matrix
with complex elements****

120 ?"Enter the matrix order"

130 input n

132 DIM inv1(n,n):DIM inv2(n,n)

135 DIM b1(n,n):DIM b2(n,n):DIM x1(n,n):DIM
x2(n,n)

137 DIM z1(n,n):DIM z2(n,n)

140 DIM a1(n,n):DIM a2(n,n)

145 DIM a(n,n):DIM b(n,n):DIM x4(n,n)

150 for i=1 to n
```

160 for j=1 to n

170 ?"type element in row";i;"column";j;"Real part"

180 input a1(i,j)

190 ?"type element in row";i;"column";j;"Imaginary part"

200 input a2(i,j)

205 z1(i,j)=a1(i,j):z2(i,j)=a2(i,j)

207 REM input matrix real part in a1(), imaginary part in a2()

208 REM input matrix "   stored in z1(),   " in z2()

210 next j

220 next i

350 ?"Matrix to be inverted is;"

360 ?:?

370 for i=1 to n

380 for j=1 to n

390 ? a1(i,j);" j";a2(i,j);" ";

400 next j

410 ?

420 next i

425 ?:?"calculating..."

427 REM evaluate determinant of input matrix

430 gosub 1000

440 d1(1,1)=x1(1,1):d2(1,1)=x2(1,1)

450 REM CALCULATE ELEMENTS OF
ADJOINT MATRIX

460 for u=1 to n

470 for v=1 to n

480 for s=1 to n-1

490 x=s

500 for t=1 to n-1

510 y=t

515 REM 'cross out' row and column of input matrix

520 if t>=v then y=t+1

530 if s>=u then x=s+1

540 REM Build cofactor u,v of input matrix

550 a1(s,t)=z1(x,y):a2(s,t)=z2(x,y)

560 next t

570 next s:if n=2 then x1(1,1)=a1(s-1,t-1):x2(1,1)=a2(s-1,t-1):goto 600

580 REM Evaluate cofactor (determinant) element u,v

585 REM transpose element, divide by value of input matrix determinant

587 REM and assign sign

590 n=s-1:gosub 1000:n=s

595 REM inv1(), inv2() contain the real, imaginary elements of inverse

600inv1(v,u)=(1)^(u+v)*((x1(1,1)*d1(1,1)+x2(1,1)*d2(1,1))/(d1(1,1)*d1(1,1)+d2(1,1)*d2(1,1)))

610 inv2(v,u)=(-1)^(u+v)*((x2(1,1)*d1(1,1)-d2(1,1)*x1(1,1))/(d1(1,1)*d1(1,1)+d2(1,1)*d2(1,1)))

620 next v

640 next u

650 ?:?:?"Inverse matrix is;":?:?

655 for i=1 to n:for j=1 to n

660 ? inv1(i,j);" j";inv2(i,j);" ";

665 next j:?:next i

667 ?

670 ?"check by multiplying input matrix by its calculated inverse;"

675 input a$

680 ?

685 for i=1 to n:for j=1 to n

690 a(i,j)=inv1(i,j)

695 b(i,j)=z1(i,j)

700 next j:next i

710 gosub 5000:gosub 6000

715 for i=1 to n:for j=1 to n

720 b2(i,j)=b1(i,j)

725 a(i,j)=inv2(i,j)

```
730 next j:next i

735 gosub 5000:gosub 6000

740 for i=1 to n:for j=1 to n

745 a1(i,j)=b1(i,j)

750 a(i,j)=inv1(i,j)

755 next i:next j

760 for i=1 to n:for j=1 to n

765 b(i,j)=z2(i,j)

770 next j:next i

775 gosub 5000:gosub 6000

780 for i=1 to n:for j=1 to n

785 a2(i,j)=b1(i,j)

790 a(i,j)=inv2(i,j)
```

795 next j:next i

800 gosub 5000:gosub 6000

805 for i=1 to n:for j=1 to n

810 x4(i,j)=b1(i,j)

815 next j:next i

825 for i=1 to n:for j=1 to n

830 ? b2(i,j)-x4(i,j);" j";a1(i,j)+a2(i,j);" ";

835 next j

840 ?

845 next i

850 stop

1000 REM evaluates a determinant

1010 x1=1:x2=1

1020 for k=n-1 to 1 step -1

1025 gosub 4000

1030 REM *CONDENSE DETERMINANT TO NEXT LOWER ORDER*

1035 REM x1(),x2() hold elements of condensed determinant

1040 for i=1 to k

1050 for j=1 to k

1060 x1(i,j)=a1(1,1)*a1(i+1,j+1)-
a2(1,1)*a2(i+1,j+1)-
a1(i+1,1)*a1(1,j+1)+a2(i+1,1)*a2(1,j+1)

1070
x2(i,j)=a2(1,1)*a1(i+1,j+1)+a2(i+1,j+1)*a1(1,1)-
a2(i+1,1)*a1(1,j+1)-a2(i,j+1)*a1(i+1,1)

1080 next j

1090 next i

1095 y1(1,1)=1:y2(1,1)=0

184

```basic
1100 if k>1 then gosub 2000

1102 gosub 3000

1105 next k

1140 x1(1,1)=x1*x1(1,1):x2(1,1)=x2*x2(1,1)

1150 return

2000 REM*calculate ((a1(1,1)+ja2(1,1))^(k-1)*

2002 a=a1(1,1):b=a2(1,1)

2003 a3(1,1)=1:a4(1,1)=0

2010 for i=1 to k-1

2020 c=a3(1,1):d=a4(1,1)

2030 a3(1,1)=c*a-d*b

2040 a4(1,1)=d*a+c*b

2060 next i

2070 a=y1(1,1)
```

2071 REM *calculate (y1(1,1)+jy2(1,1)/(a()^(k-1))

2072 y1(1,1)=a3(1,1)/(a3(1,1)^2+a4(1,1)^2)

2074 y2(1,1)=-a4(1,1)/(a3(1,1)^2+a4(1,1)^2)

2080 gosub 8000

2100 return

3000 REM*put x() back in a()*

3010 for i=1 to k

3020 for j=1 to k

3025 if k>1 then gosub 7000

3030 a1(i,j)=x1(i,j)

3040 a2(i,j)=x2(i,j)

3050 next j

3060 next i

```
3070 return

4000 REM SWOP ROWS FOR LARGEST PIVOT

4010 for m=1 to k

4020 if abs(a1(1,1))>abs(a1(1+m,1)) then 4200

4030 x1=x1*-1:x2=x2*-1

4040 for l=1 to k+1

4050 b1(1,l)=a1(1,l):b2(1,l)=a2(1,l)

4060 a1(1,l)=a1(1+m,l):a2(1,l)=a2(1+m,l)

4070 a1(1+m,l)=b1(1,l):a2(1+m,l)=b2(1,l)

4080 next l

4200 next m

4210 return

5000 for i=1 to n:for j=1 to n

5010 b1(i,j)=0
```

5020 next j:next i:return

6000 for k=1 to n:for i=1 to n:for j=1 to n

6010 b1(i,k)=b1(i,k)+a(i,j)*b(j,k)

6020 next j:next i:next k:return

7000 a=x1(i,j)

7030 x1(i,j)=x1(i,j)*y1(1,1)-x2(i,j)*y2(1,1)

7040 x2(i,j)=x2(i,j)*y1(1,1)+_y2(1,1)*a

7050 return

8000 r=SQR(y1(1,1)^2+y2(1,1)^2)

8010 if y1(1,1)<0 then y2(1,1)=-y2(1,1)

8015 if abs(y1(1,1)/r)<0.0000001 then th=3.141593/(2*k):goto 8030

8020 th=y1(1,1)/r:th=th/SQR(1-th*th)/th:th=ATN(th)/k

8030 a=r^(1/k)*cos(th)

8035 if abs(y2(1,1)/r)>0.999999 then
th=3.141593/(2*k)*SGN(y2(1,1)):goto 8050

8040 th=y2(1,1)/r:th=th/SQR(1-
th*th):th=ATN(th)/k

8050 b=r^(1/k)*sin(th)

8060 of y1(1,1)>=0 then 8090

8070
a1=cos(3.141593/k):b1=sin(3.141593/k):a2=a1*a-
b1*b:b2=b1*a+b*a1

8080 y1(1,1)=a2:y2(1,1)=b2:goto 8100

8090 y1(1,1)=a:y2(1,1)=b

8100 return

APPENDIX 9: PRINT-OUT OF THE SIMULTANEOUS EQUATION-SOLVING PROGRAM IN *BASIC*

100 REM *** solves simultaneous equations of order n ***

110 ?:?:?

120 ?"Equations to be solved must be in the form,":?:?

130 ?"   a* u1 + b* u2 + c* u3 +...+ k* un = constant"

140 ?:?:?:?

150 ?:?"where u1, u2, u3,..., un are the unknowns"

160 ?:?:?:?:?:?

170 ?"type in the number of unknowns (must equal the number of rows);"

180 input n:?

190 dim u(n,1):dim p(n,1)

200 dim a(n,n):dim x(n,n):x=1

210 dim k(n,1):dim z(n,n):dim b(n,n)

220 for i=1 to n

230 for j=1 to n

240 ?"input the coefficient of the unknown in row";i;"column";j

250 input a(i,j)

260 REM* hold det a() in z() *

270 z(i,j)=a(i,j)

280 next j:next i

290 for i=1 to n

300 ?"input the constant in row";i

310 inputk(i,1)

320 next i:?:?

330 ?"the equations to be solved are;"

340 ?

350 for i=1 to n

360 for j=1 to n

370 ?z(i,j);"*u";j,

380 next j

390 ?"=";k(i,1)

400 next i

410 gosub 680:d=x(1,1)

420 REM*d contains the value of det a()*

430 gosub 1000

440 ?:?"the solutions are;":?

450 for t=1 to n

460 for s=1 to n

470 REM*replace column t of det a() with the equation constants in k()*

480 a(s,t)=k(s,1)

490 next s

500 REM*evaluate resulting determinant*

520 gosub 680

530 REM*x(1,1) contains the value*

540 ?" u";t;"=";x(1,1)/d;" ";

550 u(t,1)=x(1,1)/d

560 gosub 1000

570 next t

580 ?:?

590 ?"check solutions by substituting in the equations (y/n)?"

600 input a$:if a$="y" then ?:?:?"right hand sides are;":?:goto 620

```
610 ?:?:?:stop

620 for i=1 to n

630 for j=1 to n

640 p(i,1)=p(i,1)+z(i,j)*u(j,1)

650 next j

660 ?p(i,1)

670 next i:?:stop

680 REM*evaluates a determinant by
condensation*

681 x=1

690 for k=n-1 to 1 step -1

700 gosub 880

710 for i=1 to k

720 for j=1 to k
```

730 REM*next lower order determinant is in x()*

740 x(i,j)=a(1,1)*a(i+1,j+1)-a(i+1,1)*a(1,j+1)

750 next j

760 next i

780 gosub 820

790 next k

792 x(1,1)=x*x(1,1)

795 return

810 REM*put det x() back in a()*

820 y=1/a(1,1)^(k-1):x=x*SGN(y)

825 for i=1 to k

830 for j=1 to k

832 if k>1 then x(i,j)=x(i,j)*(SGN(y)*y)^(1/k)

840 a(i,j)=x(i,j)

850 next j

860 next i

870 return

880 for n=1 to k

890 REM*swop rows for largest a(?,1)*

900 if abs(a(1,1))>abs(a(1+m,1)) then 980

910 REM* if rows swopped, reverse determinant sign*

920 x=x*-1

930 for l=1 to k+1

940 b(1,l)=a(1,l)

950 a(1,l)=a(1+m,l)

960 a(1+m,l)=b(1,l)

970 next l

```
980 next m

990 return

1000 for i=1 to n

1010 REM*restore det a()*

1020 for j=1 to n

1030 a(i,j)=z(i,j)

1040 next j

1050 next i

1060 return
```

APPENDIX 10: PRINT-OUT OF THE POLYNOMIAL EQUATION-SOLVING PROGRAM IN *BASIC*

```
100 ?"input the order of the polynomial"

110 input n

120 n1=n

130 REM*n1 holds the order of f(x)*

140 dim n2(n+1):dim r(n+1):dim r1(n+1)

150 REM*n2() holds the coefficients of f(x)*

160 dim a(n+1):n1(n+1):dim c(n):dim b(3)

170 for i=n+1 to 1 step -1

180 ?"input the coefficient of x^";i-1

190 input a(i)

200 n1(i)=a(i)
```

210 n2(i)=a(i)

220 next i:?:?

230 ?"calculating roots...":?:?

240 for h=1 to n1

250 REM*evaluate root and divide polynomial n1 times*

260 gosub 480

270 REM* go to root evaluation subroutine*

280 if abs(a)<0.0000001 then a=0

290 if abs(b)<0.0000001 then b=0:? a:r(ii)=a:ii=ii+1:jj=jj+1:got 340

300 REM*if root is real divide polynomial by x-root*

310r(ii)=a:ii=ii+1:r(ii)=a:ii=ii+1:r1(jj)=b:jj=jj+1: r1(jj)=-b:jj=jj+1:? a;"+/-";abs(b);"i"

320 if abs(b)>0 then b(3)=1:b(2)=-

2*a:b(1)=a*a+b*b:m=2:
goto 360

330 REM*if root is imaginary, divide by (x-root)(x-conj)*

340 x=1

350 b(2)=1:b(1)=-a

360 gosub 920

370 REM*goto polynomial division subroutine*

380 if m=2 then n=n-1:h=h+1

390 n=n-1:next h

400 ?:?:?"check by inserting each root into f(x), f(x)=":?

410 n=n1:for i=n+1 to 1 step -1

420 a(i)=n2(i):n1(i)=n2(i)

430 next i

440 for kk=0 to n-1:a=r(kk):b=r1(kk):gosub 780

450 ? p;q;"i":next kk

460 stop

480 a=1:b=1

490 a1=a

500 for l=1 to 300

510 REM*evaluate root by successive approximation using dx=-f(x)/f'(x)*

520 gosub 600

540 a2=a:b2=b

550 a=a-(yr*y1r+y1*y1i)/(y1r*y1r+y1i*y1i)

560 b=b-(yi*y1r-yr*y1i)/(y1r*y1r+y1i*y1i)

570 if abs(a2-a)<0.000001 and abs(b2-b)<0.000001 then return

580 next i

```
590 ?"no root found"

600 gosub 780

610 REM*evaluate f(x)*

620 yr=p:yi=q

630 for i=n to 2 step -1

640 REM*find f'(x)*

650 a(i)=n1(i+1)*i

660 next i

670 a(1)=n1(2)

680 n=n-1

690 gosub 780

691 if abs(p)<0.0000001 then p=0.1*SGN(p)

700 REM*evaluate f'(x))*
```

710 y1r=p:y1i=q

720 n=n+1

730 for i=1 to n

740 REM*restore f(x) in a()*

750 a(i)=n1(i)

760 next i

770 return

780 e=1:f=0:p=0:q=0

790 REM*evaluate polynomial subroutine*

800 for i=n+1 to 2 step -1

810 for j=i to 2 step -1

820 k=e

830 e=e*a-f*b

840 f=f*a+k*b

850 next j

860 p=p+a(i)*e

870 q=q+a9i)*f

880 e=1:f=0

900 next i

910 return

920 for i=n+1 to m step -1

930 REM*divide polynomial by x-root or (x-root)(x-conj)*

940 c(i-m)=a(n+1)/b(m+1)

950 for j=m+1 to 1 step -1

960 a(j+n-m)=a(j+n-m)-c(i-m)*b(j)

970 next j

980 gosub 1050

990 REM*goto subroutine to shift a(k-1) of quotient into a(k)*

1000 next i

1010 for i=n-m+1 to 1 step -1

1020 a(i)=c(i):n1(i)=c(i)

1030 next i

1040 return

1050 for k=n+1 to 2 step -1

1060 REM*shift a(k-1) into a(k)*

1070 a(k)=a(k-1)

1080 next k

1090 return

BIBLIOGRAPHY & REFERENCES

(1989) TurboC v2.01
http://www.borland.co.uk (accessed 5/7/2011)

Kopnicky, L. (2011b)

http://www.vintage-
basic.net/downloads/Vintage_BASIC

(accessed 3/1/2014)

Philips, A. (1998) *Programmer's File Editor*
Lancaster University Computer Centre
http://www.lancaster.ac.uk

Trigger, P. (2013) *Mathematical Methods for
Engineering Science* Durham, KDP
ISBN 97814946815660

(2000) Microprocessor-based
Computers. Block 2 Program development and the
C language *T223 Technology: A Level 2 Course*
The Open University